Introduction to the Pastoral Epistles

Edgar (Ted) Stubbersfield

ISBN: 0992425905
ISBN-13: 978-0-9924259-0-6

DEDICATION

This book is dedicated to my friends and former pastors, John and Jeanette Simmons.

CONTENTS

Abbreviations i

1 Authorship Pg 1

2 Historical Background Pg 17

3 The Purpose of each Letter Pg 32

4 The Ephesian Heresy Pg 45

5 Imperial Cult Pg 72

6 Opinion of Unbelievers Pg 87

7 Eschatology and the Pastorals Pg 81

8 Church Officers Pg 84

9 Works Cited Pg 119

ABBREVIATIONS

BDAG	Bauer-Danker Lexicon
JETS	Journal of the Evangelical Theological Society
JSOT	Journal for the Study of the Old Testament
NEB	New English Bible

.

1. AUTHORSHIP

The purpose and interpretation of the Pastoral Epistles cannot be considered apart from the difficult matter of authorship. The subject of authorship also brings uncomfortable questions about the traditional understanding of Biblical authority. Hundreds of millions of Christians are oblivious to and would care nothing for questions of who wrote the First and Second Timothy and Titus as, for most, the question of canonicity and authority is the same. They believe these books to be the inspired and revealed word of God and helpful for Christian living. For the Catholic Church "the criterion of canonicity is acceptance into the Vulgate" (Brown 1966, 336). Acceptance by Jerome would not be sufficient for the Protestants who require different criteria. For many the sole criterion is simply whether it is part of the King James Bible (Brown 1966, 336). Others, who are informed about the problems of authorship, are content to let the matter rest with church confessions.[1] For others the questions is meaningless, or even an affront to Christianity as talk of any "preconceived notion of "inspiration" … will not bear examination when confronted with the facts" (Guy 1968, 2).

The Epistles claim to be written by Paul but this is far from universally accepted now. It is claimed that non Pauline authorship is the view held by 80-90%[2] of modern scholars. Though some hold for a date of authorship of c. A.D. 70, (Gill 2008, 75) the date generally given is about A.D. 80-100 (Brown 1997, 668). While the traditional view still has its supporters, the prevailing opinion is that the letters as they stand, were composed by some "Pauline enthusiast" (Kelly 1981, 4-5) and derive from the sub-apostolic age, perhaps even as late as the middle of the second century. Non Pauline authorship is said to be one of the "assured results of

---

[1] "I am aware of the problems of authorship but as a Lutheran pastor I am obliged to believe that the letters are Paul's" (Liebelt *Pers. Com.* 2006)

[2] Mounce asserts that scholarship is changing and that a "significant number of commentaries in English in the last twenty years hold to Pauline authorship" (2000, xlviii)

scholarship" (Mounce 2000, lxxxiv), so assured that when the NEB translates 1 Timothy 1:2, it refers to Timothy as "his trueborn son". Certainly, the second century, with inefficient "church organisation, the menace of sects, the undermining of the authority of the Old Testament and the misuse of Paul (by Marcion)" (Guthrie 1990, 621) is a setting that could have encouraged such a book to be written. If the works were written too soon after the death of Timothy and Titus, their fraudulent claims would be recognized so a late date is necessary (Gill 2008, 76).

Writing under the name of another (pseudonymity) is said to be perfectly acceptable (Dunn 2000, 779) if not indeed common about this time, so this charge has to be looked at seriously. Our decision on authorship will determine how we understand the core of the letters. The second letter fits the mould of a Pauline letter down to a claimed loose train of thought that can be typical of Paul[3]. If the second book is pseudonymous there is no obvious reason for writing such a work (Dibelius and Conzelmann 1972, 1). The real problem lies with 1 Timothy. Paul does not write to the church as he otherwise does. Much of its content could well be meant for others as it shows the transference (Mounce 2000, lix) of apostolic authority to anyone who questioned Timothy's actions in correcting and reorganising the church. In this way it acts like "royal correspondence". This is a document where the delegate's authority is established and the will of a superior for the community is communicated (Johnson 2001, 137-41). This type of letter also set the code of practice for the delegates conduct and set the limits of the delegate's authority. As such it would the basis of an appeal to the leader if the delegates conduct did not match that laid out in the letter (Johnson 2001, 141).

In the light of future heresies, reasons can be put forward for fabricating the book. Titus fits somewhere in the middle which is not surprising if his church was not as well developed as appears to be the case.

---

[3] Dibelelius and Conzelmannn give Rom. 12 and Col. 3&4 as examples (1972, 1)

The objections of the critics focus around the following arguments:

(i). The vocabulary of the Pastoral Epistles is very similar to each other, but very different from the other 10 epistles normally attributed to Paul.[4]

○ Paul used the word "spirit" 80 times in other 10 epistles traditionally attributed to him but it is only used 3 times here.
○ He does not use characteristic words like "blood", "uncircumcised" and "works of the Law".
○ There are 306 new words[5] not found in the other Pauline works (Carson 1992, 360).[6]
○ There is an absence of particles, pronouns and prepositions. (Moumce 2000, xcviii).

(ii). The style of the Pastoral Epistles betrays their forged origin; they only remind us of Paul.

○ Words common to the 10 other letters of the Pauline corpus and to the Pastorals have different meanings. It is said that faith in the 10 is subjective trust but here it is what is believed distilled in the form of "faithful sayings" (Guthrie, 190. 619).

(iii). The theology is not Pauline.

   ○ Undue stress is placed on good works.
   ○ The cross is no longer central (Mounce 2000, lxxxix)
   ○ The work of the Spirit is not emphasised (Guthrie 1990, 618)
   ○ The Fatherhood of God is not present (Guthrie 1990, 630)

---

[4] Many New Testament scholars, perhaps the majority of those who reject the Pauline authorship of the Pastoral Epistles, also reject his authorship of other books in the Pauline cannon.

[5] The argument seems to be limiting Paul's vocabulary to 2,177 words, the total of the ten other epistles (Carson 1992, 361). The vocabulary of a first century scholar would have to have been broad.

[6] Carson's and Guthrie's view must be modified as not all scholars agree that the 10 books in question were all actually authored by Paul.

° The believer's mystical union with Christ is not stressed (Guthrie 190, 618)

° The concept of God is partly Jewish, partly Hellenistic (Guthrie, 1957, 40)

(iv). They refer to Marcionism, a second century Gnosticism. Marcion was excommunicated in A.D. 144.

- ° The heresy described matches 2nd century Marcionism
- ° The writer actually refers to the title of Marcion's book Antithesis in 1 Tim 6:20.

(v). They reveal a marked advance in ecclesiastical organisation far beyond the time of Paul

° It is said that there was no official ministry in Paul's day but here we see elders serving under one bishop.[7] (Von Campenhausen 1969, 7)

(vi). The Acts record cannot be cited to support the ministry of Timothy and Titus. Paul was only imprisoned in Rome once and was put to death at the end of it. The journeys alluded to in the Pastorals are impossible.

The Theological Problem Examined

The strongest argument for in-authenticity is theological, not historical. If the theology can be shown to be contrary to or different from the 10, the case must be considered proven. There must be room of course for a development of theology which is different.

Of the significant number of words, perhaps as many as 175 that are used only once in the Pastorals, and the 130 non-Pauline words

---

[7] Elders are "a fundamentally different way of thinking about the Church, which can only with difficulty be combined with the with the Pauline picture of the congregation, and certainly cannot be derived from it" (Von Campenhausen 1969, 71).

most are known to be common at the traditional date for writing (Gill 2008, 74). The simple use of an amanuensis At the core of the argument is a statistical analysis of the word use which requires an "artificial and wooden construction" based around what scholars think Paul should or should not have spoken about (Mounce 2000, lxxxix). This leaves little room for a creative writer writing to his two closest associates who knew his teaching and passion intimately.

A theme in one Pauline book can be completely missing or of minimal interest in another whereas a concept common to other books can be expressed in totally different words. The one saving act could be referred to as justification, redemption, reconciliation, ransom, cleansing and propitiation (Fee 1995, 15).

	Rom	1 Cor	2 Cor	Gal	Eph	Phil	Col	1 Thess	2 Thess	Phlm
Verse count	432	437		149	155	104		89	47	
Word count	7114	6842		2233	2423	1631		1482	823	
To justify	15	2	0	8	0	0	0	0	0	0
Root for just, righteous	63	4	7	13	4	6	1	1	0	0
Righteousness of God	8	0	1	0	0	0	0	0	0	0
Root for cross	0	6	1	6	1	2	2	0	0	0
Uncircumcision	11	2	0	3	1	0	2	0	0	0
Son (of Jesus)	7	2	1	4	1	0	1	1	0	0
Freedom	1	1	1	4	0	0	0	0	0	0
Flesh	26	11	11	18	9	5	9	0	0	1
Flesh vs spirit	13	1	1	7	0	0	1	0	0	0
Law	74	9	0	32	1	3	0	0	0	0

Table 1, Analysis of key themes in recognised Pauline epistles (Mounce 2000, xc)

The table shows clearly the clumped nature of occurrences of key Pauline themes in the ten epistles attributed to him (Mounce 2000, xc). A statistical approach to authorship is inadequate as the number of occurrences of a word is seen to be totally dependant on its historical and theological context (Mounce 2000, xc).

Mounce's contention that, if major themes can be missing from 1 and 2 Thessalonians, then they can be missing from the Pastorals as well, is reasonable. (2000, xc). The statistical approach is no absolute guide to Paul's theology either. We only know how important he viewed communion from 1 Corinthians. Without that book it would be claimed that his churches did not know of the sacraments (Mounce 2000, xc). Some of these epistles show themes occurring only once so "it can hardly be classified as a theme in that epistle; and if it is not a theme, then it could be a passing comment, which is only slightly different to an omission" (Mounce 20000, xci).

Part of the authorship question revolves around the emphasis of themes such as piety. If this argument is accepted then Romans would also have to be suspect as the theme "righteousness of God" is almost totally found in that book. The presence of new themes or absence of old ones proves nothing.

The minimal use of Spirit (once in each book) is said to be a clear indication of in-authenticity – (Mounce 2000, xci). By this argument, half of the ten would be questionable. The spirit is central to theology of the church in the creeds (1 Tim 3:16; Titus 3:5-6). The Spirit's power is also personal as the strength to achieve his task does not come from within 2 Tim. 1:6. Timothy calling was first confirmed by prophetic statements (1 Tim 4:14) and then established through the empowering of the spirit (1 Tim. 1:18; 4:14; 2 Tim 1:6-7).

Examples of words and phrases which are said to be used differently or in a contradictory way are in Christ, faith and righteousness. This is only an issue if a multiple meaning is contradictory to Paul's practices in other letters or if the usage in the Pastorals is not a logical development of previous thought or, there is just a simple shift of emphasis.[8]

The problem with this line of argument is the arguments are

---

[8] Mounce gives an example of possible growth of Paul's theology in the Pastorals is applying the title "saviour" to both Jesus and God (2000, xciv).

extremely subjective. Paul calls himself a blasphemer and an evil doer (1 Tim. 1:13) yet Dibelius and Conzelmann assert that on the basis of Phil 3:4ff it is inconceivable that Paul would use this expression of his past self (1972, 28). It may not have been the view of him within Judaism at the time he was the apostle of the Law but it was certainly the message from the vision of Christ on the Damascus road. Another example is the argument that the "just" person in 1 Tim 1:9 is stoic (Mounce 2000, xcii) but a just person being someone saved by faith is in keeping with Paul.

Mounce maintains that there are differences of emphasis which is to be expected due to the circumstances but that for every occurrence "there are likely interpretations that are in line with Pauline usage elsewhere" (Mounce 2000, xciv). To establish that a Paul can use a word with a variety of meanings, he gives the example of "faith". It can be used of the Christian faith (2 Cor. 13:5, Gal. 1:23, Phil. 1:27). The faith of the Romans that is proclaimed throughout the world (Rom 1:8) is the fact that they are Christians (Mounce 2000, xcii). Faith (pistis) can also have a concrete meaning such as pledge, evidence and the clear basis of faith (Hay 1989, 461) Mounce 2000, xcii). Righteousness, likewise is not a simple single meaning as it is both gift and responsibility, and without the latter it is reasonable to question the existence of the former (Fee 1987, 143).

What are the implications for accepting pseudonymity when nine of the New Testament books are either anonymous or vaguely identified? Whereas the message of the anonymous books stand even if our understanding of the author was is in error, the Pastorals are different as they claim Pauline authorship i.e. they may be built on a lie. Brown puts the matter clearly "It is hard to see, however, how a proposal that the writer of the Pastorals was intentionally deceptive and consciously desired to counteract[9] Paul's genuine heritage can be fitted into any notion of inspiration, even a sophisticated one" (1997, 667-8). Critics of Pauline

---

[9] Some radical authorship theories see the writer correcting the Pauline heritage (Brown 1997, 663)

authorship refer to the writer as an imitator or a devout Paulinist and studiously avoid the word forger with its moral stigma as it is said to prejudice the issue (Guthrie 1990, 645-6). Attempts are made to sanitise the motives of the writer by claiming that it would almost have been an injustice to call the thoughts of Paul by the real author's name (Guthrie 1990, 645). It is further claimed that the church was aware of their origin and that their pseudonymous origin was only lost to later generations (Marshall 1999, 92). There is no empirical evidence to justify this assertion so it remains an unproven claim

Brown speculates that even with pseudonymity it may be possible to accept inspiration and still reject revelation. This is much the same as interpreting historical narrative where the story is generally told with no comment. We are left to make up our own mind if it is a good or bad example (Fee 1979, 60). In the same way we are to make up our own mind about what is said in the Pastorals. Do they show a system "destructive of the personal worth of women" (Brown 1997, 668)? If these books do show repression and if the books are revealed then we also can oppress women: in fact it becomes our duty to do so. If it is just an inspired document we can learn from it that God does not want us to oppress women because it is not in his nature to do so. Such an understanding of the Pastorals would cause us to be more careful about framing the church in the social setting it is found (Brown 1997, 668).

On the face these charges seem conclusive to many, but Fee sees the argument against a pseudographer as hinging on two points. Firstly the letters make sense in the historical setting in the context they are claimed to be set and secondly, no critic can give a satisfactory answer for writing three books (Fee 1985, 142). Many of the claims do not bear close scrutiny. For example of the 306 different words used in the pastoral and not found in the other 10 epistles, only 9 are common to each other Pastoral. If the same logic is applied a different writer must be posed for each of the 3 Pastorals. It is only a minority that see them as not coming from the same author (Brown 1997, 673). The theology has also been clearly shown to be the same, e.g. faith has the dual meanings in the ten as in the Pastorals.

One of the standard approaches to pseudonymity occurs in Dibelius and Conzelmann's The Pastoral Epistles (1972, 1-10). However, the logical framework of their argument seems faulty. They admit that there is no single overarching argument that must demand that 1 and 2 Timothy are not Pauline. For Dibelius and Conzelmann their conclusion depends on "the convergence of a whole series of arguments" (Dibelius and Conzelmann, 1972, 1). For them one of the strongest in this "series of arguments" is the language of the Pastorals. They reject the statistical approach to the language as inadequate (Dibelius and Conzelmann, 1972, 2) but claim the new words have more in common with the literature of Hellenistic Greek[10] than does the rest of the New Testament (Dibelius and Conzelmann, 1972, 2-3). Yet they concede that alternate theories such as a fragmentary or secretary hypotheses can explain most of this phenomenon (Dibelius and Conzelmann, 1972, 4).

The argument against Pauline authorship of the Pastorals which says that we do not read of Paul's release in Acts, therefore Paul did not have a fourth missionary journey, is a circular argument from silence. Opponents of the Pauline authorship would argue that postulating a second imprisonment is only an attempt to defend Pauline authorship. But on the basis of the Acts account, release is the only outcome to be expected. It appeared to be a case outside of the Roman legal system (Acts 25:20). Agrippa had said Paul could have been released if he had not appealed to Caesar (Acts 26:32). The generous terms of Paul's imprisonment also strongly point to release as being the expected outcome of his appeal. The prison epistles also speak of Paul's anticipated imminent release (Phm. 22; Phil. 1:25, 2:23-4). If Paul was not released from the imprisonment of Acts, as asserted by Dibelius

---

[10] This is refuted by Guthrie who claims virtually all the words that occur once (hapaxes) in the Pastorals are known in Greek literature by the middle of the first century and half are in the Septuagint which Paul would have been intimately acquainted with. A considerable number of the "new" Pauline words are found other books of the New Testament (1990, 634-5).

and Conzelmann (1972, 3), then the events alluded to in the Pastorals must be false.

Support for their view is claimed from Acts which they maintain is only interested in Rome and that the goal of evangelising the world is satisfied with simply reaching Rome (Dibelius and Conzelmann, 1972, 3). This writer cannot see how support from Acts can be claimed. When writing Acts, Luke is concerned only with the spread of Christianity to Rome but this not the whole picture of the advance of Christianity. Paul was well aware that there was half an empire with good communications west of Rome and in his own writings, which must reflect his heart better than his friend Luke, speaks of an intense burden to take the gospel to areas where no one has proclaimed it before Rom. 15:20-29. This was not Rome, it was Spain.[11] To the contrary there are traditions that say Paul reached Spain and do so without contradicting Acts.[12]

There is not one early church tradition that says Paul died at the end of his first and only imprisonment without being released (Mounce 2000, lvi). Clement refers (5:7) to Paul preaching the gospel to the whole world and travelling to the extreme limit of the west.[13] The church historian Eusebius and the Muratorian fragment[14] also support this. Dibelius and Conzelmann dismiss this

---

[11] Eusebius records further preaching after a first Roman imprisonment Ecclesiastical History. While this fourth century work may just reflect an earlier error, with his access to much more material than we have as in 3.1.2 he refers to basing his history of the death of Peter and Paul on a lost work of Oregin. Guthrie comments "traditional opinion may well preserve more truth" than allowed by the critics (1957, 21). Even if trip to Spain is disputed it is a strong indication of a release from the Acts 28 imprisonment.

[12] The agreed Pauline works contain travels and events that we know nothing of from the record of Acts including shipwrecks, beatings and imprisonments, 2 Cor. 11:23-27.

[13] Clement could still have had members that would have witnessed Paul's imprisonment and execution. (Mounce 2000, lv).

[14] The fragment, possibly written about 220 AD was found by the Italian historian Muratori C. 1740. It gives a list of books which were for the edification of the church and those which were Apostolic. The later could be read in church. It listed 22 of the 27 present New Testament. It gave information about each book, its author and its historical background.

record except for Clement, who it is claimed, is in agreement with them (Dibelius and Conzelmann, 1972, 3). But Clement certainly is not in agreement. Writing from Rome to Corinth, Clement talks of what happened to Paul "after preaching both in the east and west". Rome it must be conceded is west of Jerusalem but Rome is not west of Rome but Spain is (similarly Mounce 2000, lv).

While Dibelius and Conzelmann suggest that a genuine letter would have been written to the church (1972, 1), there is no reason why Paul could not and indeed should not have written private letters to Timothy and Titus. Dibelius and Conzelmann provide no satisfying explanation for their assertion that the precision in a personal letter is not to be of the level that is found in a letter to a church. For instance in 2 Timothy, the author talks about his first defence and Dibelius and Conzelmann argue that this is proof that there could not have been a second imprisonment (1972, 3). Obviously with two imprisonments it would not be strictly his first defence but possibly his fourth or fifth overall. But in the context of a personal letter to a friend who was aware of what was occurring, this would have made perfect sense. It is agreed that the author knows Acts[15] (Dibelius and Conzelmann 1972, 3). Therefore, if 2 Timothy is pseudonymous and not written for Timothy's benefit, why was this obvious discrepancy written? If this verse is accepted as authoritative in building a case and claim that first is the absolute first, then it demands Pauline authorship as it is within the context of a known imprisonment. Why, when the Pastorals bear the mark of "historical particularity" are personal reminiscences not linked into the Acts history (Carson 1992, 363)?

Dibelius and Conzelmann recognise that 2Timothy "seems to be a genuine personal communication" (Dibelius and Conzelmann, 1972, 7) to Timothy full of Paul's personal idiosyncrasies (Dibelius and Conzelmann, 1972, 7). However, despite 2

---

[15] Brown claims that "in atmosphere and vocabulary the Pastorals are very close to Luke-Acts, to the point that some have thought that the same person wrote them" (New York, 666). As Brown puts the date of Acts during the 80's this requires a date after Paul Death for composition (New York, 666).

Timothy's appearance as genuine,[16] they can elicit no reason why a fraudulent work would be written (Dibelius and Conzelmann, 1972, 2-3). Despite this, it is claimed quite categorically "to be sure, the Pastorals are pseudonymous" (Dibelius and Conzelmann, 1972, 7).

They argue that, because 1 Timothy is considered by them to be pseudonymous, and because 1 and 2 Timothy had the same author, then 2 Timothy must be pseudonymous also. It seems just as valid to argue that, because there is no convincing case against a Pauline authorship for 2 Timothy, and because the argument against a Pauline authorship of 1 Timothy is particularly weak, then their admittedly mutual author would most likely be Paul.

Dibelius and Conzelmann start with the problems and interpret the whole in light of these problems. This approach is very different to exegeting the text in its totality, so that the significant and new in the text can be understood in the light of the evolution of the Pauline churches.[17] For example, fundamental changes had occurred in Paul's approach to the leadership of the churches for very understandable reasons, as will be argued later. 2 Timothy was written within Paul's life because of the absence of any hint in succession of the episcopos. There is no hint of a "ritual of establishment and succession" (Dibelius and Conzelmann 1972, 8) with the laying on of hands in 2 Tim. 1:6.

Many scholars hold that, beyond the lifespan of Paul, the Gentile church was devoid of a structured two level form of church government, They argue that we read very little about church officers in the recognised Pauline epistles. They see the "exclusion

---

[16] Far from being an obvious literary fraud, in all the Pastorals "there are many passages that give the impression of imitation" (Dibelius and Conzelmannn, 1972, 4). Theories exist that assume only I Timothy and Titus are not genuine. Refer to Marshall, I. Howard. *The Pastoral Epistles*,.(London: T&T Clark, 1999) 86

[17] Dibelius and Conzelmannn cite Hans Van Campenhausen *Ecclesiastical Authority and Spiritual Power* (1969,106-119) to justify the un-Pauline character of church order in the Pastorals (1972, 3). I accept the order is different but that does not prove pseudonymity.

on principle of all formal authority within the individual congregation" (Von Campenhausen 1969, 70). If this is right, Acts and the Pastoral Epistles must be rejected as non authentic (Von Campenhausen 1969, 77, 30). The system of church government that we see in the Pastorals is supposed to originate at a "degenerate" time in church history (Von Campenhausen 1969, 80). During the time in which the Pastorals are set "There is no need for "rules and regulations and prohibitions [as] the Spirit [is] the organizing principal of Christian congregations" (Von Campenhausen 1969, 58).

There is however early attestation outside of the New testament to the two level structure of church government that is seen as regressive. We see a similar arrangement in the Didache15:1 (possibly dated C. 100 A.D.) and in 1 Clement 42:4,5; 44:4,5; 52;2 (C. 98A.D.). Clement is unlike Ignatius (C. 110 A.D.) who has a three level government with a single bishop at the head (Brown 1997, 666). Irenaeus another strong supporter of the role of bishops would link himself via Polycarp through to the earliest founders of the church

Better attestation by the early church to the pastorals would have solved the matter. There are apparent quotations of 1 Tim. 6:7 and 10 in Polycarp (Phil 4.1) "But the love of money is the root of all evils." Knowing, therefore, that "as we brought nothing into the world, so we can carry nothing out,"let us arm ourselves with the armour of righteousness." It is said (Dibelius and Conzelmann 1972, 1) that, because these Pastoral verses were common sayings, linkage is not proven.[18] As two verses in close proximity in 1 Timothy can be seen in one verse in Polycarp, it would work against this being a random chance. This is further strengthened with the allusion to the armour of God of Ephesians[19] strengthening the Biblical setting.

---

[18] Brown also sees the widow motif of 1 Timothy 5:3-6 in this passage from Polycarp, leading him to assess that "the evidence slightly favours the Pastorals having been written before AD 125" (1997, 665)

[19] The reference to the duties of church officers in Polycarp Phil. 5-6 also seems to be reliant on the Pastorals.

If the works were written in the second century for the benefit of the general Christian public and heretics alike, to show what Paul would have thought, the books had to have been written by someone who had "drunk deeply from the Pauline well" (Carson 1992, 360) and was acquainted with Pauline phraseology (Guthrie 1990, 641). Yet despite this familiarity with Paul's language it is argued that the imitator was not well enough acquainted with Pauline theology to include his major themes (Guthrie 1990, 641). These are some of the very doctrines being neglected in the second century heretics and needed to be restated. If writing to a trusted associate there would have been no need to mention doctrines accepted and approved by both parties. What also is difficult to explain is how such a supporter of Paul, who was appealing to his authority would include references to him being the chief of sinners (1 Tim. 1:15), a persecutor and violent man (1 Tim. 1:13), and who no one stood with in his critical hour (2 Tim. 4:16).

It was the considered opinion of the early church fathers that these books were Pauline and were widely accepted by the end of the second century. The church did not accept books as canonical without due diligence. They were aware of the linguistic problems involved in accepting Hebrews as the work of Paul yet saw no difficulty with the PE. The early church was also careful about accepting John, 1 and 2 Peter, 2 and 3 John and Jude and James. They were also aware of spurious works circulating under the names of the Apostles such as the Acts of Paul and in the case of this work strong action was taken against the author.[20] The Acts of Paul and Thecla c.170 attest indirectly to the existence of the epistles by the use of New Testament names found only in these letters. The Muratorian fragment (C.180) talks about letters forged in Paul's name, saying they cannot be received into the catholic church "for it is not fitting that gall be mixed with honey"

---

[20] Tertullian writes "But if the writings which wrongly go under Paul's name, claim Thecla's example as a licence for women's teaching and baptizing, let them know that, in Asia, the presbyter who composed that writing, as if he were augmenting Paul's fame from his own store, after being convicted, and confessing that he had done it from love of Paul, was removed" (On Baptism 17)

(Harrison 1963, 146). The only dissenting voice was from the heretics, notably Marcion[21], who disagreed with the letters' contents. The Pastoral Epistles appear to be the source for passages written by Polycarp[22] (c.100-135) Ignatius[23] (c. 110), Clement of Rome[24] (c. 95)[25] and Irenaeus[26].

Guthrie argues that there is little evidence for pseudography as an early Christian practice (1990, 608). Carson claims pseudographic letters are rare for Jews and Christians.[27] Six epistles are known but date from the fourth to the thirteenth century (1992, 367-8). Only Romans and 1 Corinthians have better attestation in the sub-apostolic age and early second century (Guthrie 1990, 608). The Pastorals are missing from the incomplete[28] third century Chester Beatty Papyri[29] but then a number of other books are also. The Pastorals were being used widely by this time so this partial document adds little to the debate (Guthrie 1990, 611).

---

[21] Marcion a contemporary of Tertullian, compiled the first known cannon of New Testament books and did not include the Pastorals in his list but he also rejected Matthew, Mark and John and severely mutilated Luke (Guthrie 1990, 609). Tertullian clearly states that he rejected these works as opposed to not being aware of them (Adv. Marc. v. 21). If they did not exist at Marcion's time what argument can be produced for their rapid acceptance?

[22] The Bishop of Smyrna who was a disciple of the Apostle John. He was martyred at the age of 86 in the year 156.

[23] The Bishop of Antioch in Syria was martyred in Rome in 115. He is remembered for seven letters he wrote to churches while under guard on his way to Rome. These letters exalt the role of the Bishop. He does not quote the Pastorals directly but uses coincidental phrases and words found elsewhere only in the Pastorals (Mounce 2000, lxvii)

[24] An early Bishop of Rome

[25] While it is argued that the Pastorals are dependant on Polycarp and Ignatius it hard to understand why an "imitator of Paul would echo the language of Ignatius and Polycarp" (Guthrie 1990, 611).

[26] Bishop of Lyon and disciple of Polycarp frequently cites the Pastoral epistles in his *Adversus Haereses* c.180and refers to them as Paul's. The heretics Irenaeus was writing against would certainly have flung back at him any hint of a doubtful provenance (Mounce 2000, lxv-lxvi).

[27] It is apparent that Carson does not consider the Gnostics to be Christians

[28] The last seven pages of the codex are missing (Mounce 2000, lxv).

[29] A collection of papyri which includes a codex of Paul's epistles (Mounce 2000, lxv)

But is there a situation where a non Pauline work can be classed as Pauline? Perhaps. A correlation may possibly be seen with Luther's Table Talks which are regarded as having been written by Luther yet he did not personally write them (T.K.T. 1999 section 1). These informal talks were given by Luther to students around his home table and some of these students took notes. After his death these notes were used to re-constitute and publish Luther's talks in his name. Such a reconstruction is not suggested but if a theory must be invoked, and there is no absolute need for one, the simplest theory should be adopted. One of the simpler theories is that, when an early collection of Paul's writings was being prepared in Ephesus, collected sayings, headings and paragraphs of Paul were edited for future generations (Marshall 1999, 1-108). With perhaps Luke writing,[30] Timothy and Titus were thus created. This theory allows for the documents to be essentially Pauline but as redacted works would allow for different linguistic styles. While this allows an early date of about 70 A.D. (Marshall 1999, 92), such a document has no life situation from which to interpret it and to give meaning to its text.

The association of Ephesus with an early collection is not unreasonable as ". . . for one momentous generation, Ephesus was the literary focus of early Christianity, and by its compilations . . . influenced Christianity more than Jerusalem, Antioch or Rome" (Goodspeed 1937, 49). This leaves a work that is authoritative, written by Paul with his self sacrificing fidelity to the apostolic mission, as remembered by disciples who shared his apostolic mission and so acquired his apostolic authority (Brown, 1997, 668).

These books are far superior to the writings of the sub-apostolic fathers and must have been written by a giant among them, but such a man is not known, especially one so devoted to Paul (Guthrie 1990, 642). Great though the works may be, without Pauline authorship and authority we must agree with Luther 1400 years later when he said "I ask for Scriptures and Eck offers me the

---

[30] It is argued that the writing style of the Pastorals reflects Acts (Moule 1965, 431).

Fathers. I ask for the sun and he shows me his lanterns. I ask: 'Where is your Scripture proof?' and he adduces Ambrose and Cyril... With all due respect to the Fathers I prefer the authority of the Scripture." Martin Luther   Great as the Pastoral Epistles may be, without genuine authorship they can have no more ultimate authority than the Acts of Paul and Thecla. Their study is of no more value than any other work by the fathers.

.

2. HISTORICAL BACKGROUND

At the end of the second missionary journey c. 52 Paul passed through the Ephesus, leaving Priscilla and Aquila to minister. Paul's friends found an Alexandrian called Apollos, who, despite teaching accurately about Jesus, knew only John's baptism. Paul later returned and ministered in Ephesus for about two years c. 52-55. When Paul arrived he found believers in Christ that had not head of the Holy Spirit and practiced John's baptism (Acts 19:1-7). Twenty years after Christ's death there was possible to find a strange mixture of accuracy and error when it came to understanding the gospel.

Paul's two year ministry was characterized by powerful preaching 19:8 and outstanding miracles 19:11-12. This led to a remarkable change in the believers as they forsook all their old ways 19:18-19. Paul's opponents would say he had led astray a large number of people here and in the whole province of Asia 19:26. The church was built and church government was established 20:17.

In c. 57 Paul passed by Ephesus and met the elders, predicted that from among the elders heresy would arise and damage the church. He went on to prison in Caesarea and Rome

The Pastorals do not fit with Paul's travels as we read in Acts, a record we know to be very incomplete (2 Cor. 11). Attempts have been made to fit these journeys into this time period with suggestions that 1 Timothy was written between 1 and 2 Corinthians and Titus being written on the last journey back to

Jerusalem. The Caesarean imprisonment was the occasion for 2 Timothy. This suggestion has never received much support (Guthrie 1990, 613). The journeys appear to have occurred beyond that time covered in Acts. This requires a second Roman imprisonment. The only independent reference to Paul being released from prison in Rome is found in I Clement 5:7 "After preaching both in the east and west, he gained the illustrious reputation due to his faith, having taught righteousness to the whole world, and come to the extreme limit of the west,[29] and suffered martyrdom under the prefects".

A possible, but not the only reconstruction[31] of the events and travels referred to the Pastorals is given below: (Hendriksen 1983, 39-40)

(i). On Paul's release from his first Roman imprisonment he sent Timothy to Philippi with the good news. Phil. 2:19-23

(ii). Paul headed for Asia Minor via Crete where he left Titus behind to complete the organisation of the churches.

(iii). Paul travelled to Ephesus, on to Colosse, Philemon 22, and returned to Ephesus.

(iv). Timothy joined Paul in Ephesus, Paul asked him to remain there

---

[29] Some think Rome, others Spain, and others even Britain, to be here referred to. [See note at end.]

[31] Refer to Elwell's Encountering the New Testament P.334 for an alternative map.

(v). Paul journeyed to Macedonia, Phil 2:24. He wanted to return to Ephesus but, as he expects to be delayed, he wrote 1 Timothy and Titus. Titus was asked to meet him at Nicopolis, Tit 3:12.

(vi). Paul travelled to Nicopolis and wintered there, Tit. 3:12 and was joined there by Titus.

(vii). Paul and possibly Titus visited Spain, Rom 15:28 & Clement of Rome (similarly Mounce 2000, lix).

(viii). Paul returned, Trophimus was left sick at Miletus near Ephesus, 2 Tim 4:20. He may have met Timothy again, 2 Tim 1:4.

(ix). Paul visited Carpus in Troas and left his cloak behind, 2 Tim 4:13 He went on to Rome via Corinth where Erastus remained, 2 Tim 4:20. It was probably in one of these cities that he was arrested.

(x). His Roman imprisonment was severe and brief. He wrote 2 Timothy asking Timothy to come to Rome.

This possible reconstruction is shown in the map following.

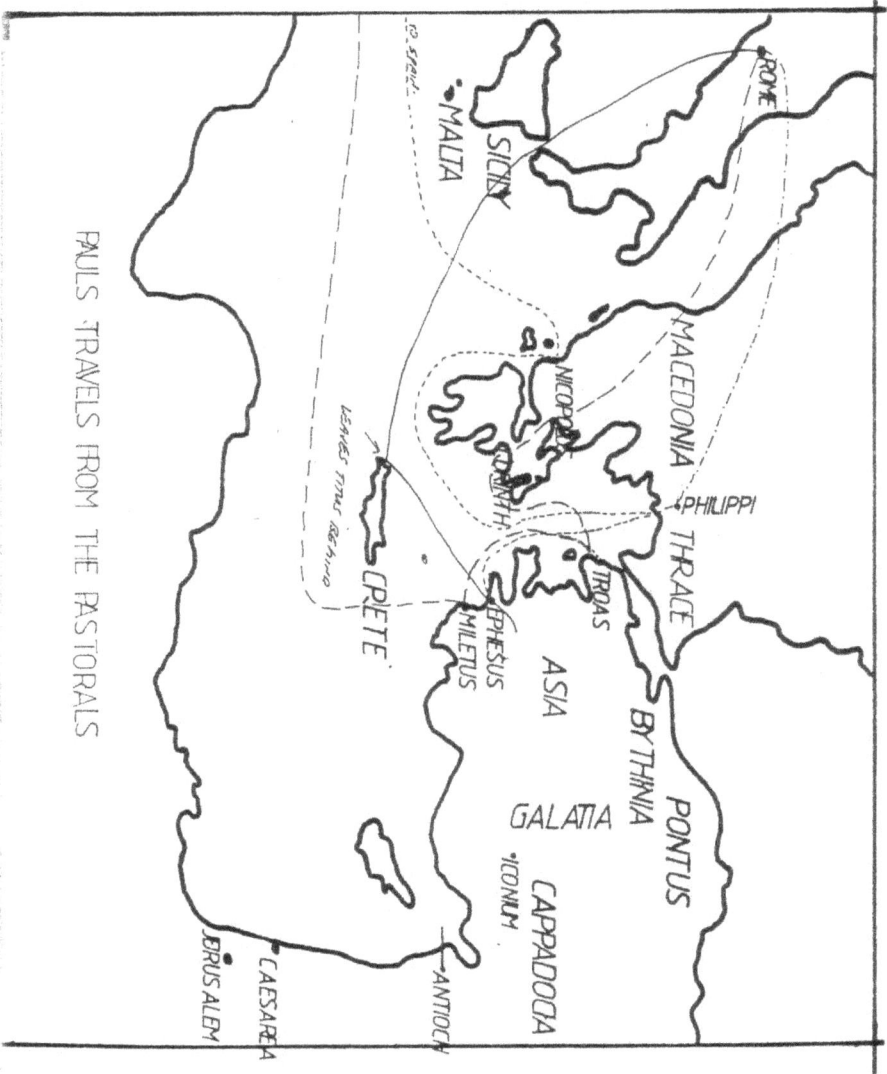

PAUL'S FOURTH MISSIONARY JOURNEY

This reconstruction sees that Paul, contrary to expectation arrived in/near Ephesus again c. 62. He left Timothy behind to sort out matters in the church.

At the time of Timothy's ministry, The Jewish foundation (Acts 18:24-26; 19:1-7) has been replaced with a church that was heavily if not predominantly Gentile (Acts 20:21, Eph. 2:11-13, 19; 3:1; 4:17-24). The church in Ephesus was in trouble with "savage wolves" doing great damage to the church (20:20), but not in the full blown form that Paul had predicted in Acts 20 and I Tim 4:1. Tradition records that John lived to an old age and eventually died in Ephesus, perhaps another 20 years on from Timothy's ministry. This long predicted falling away would happen during the time John was there during which he wrote 1 John. The name of the heretic is known, Cerinthus. The church would survive, Cerinthus with his followers departing from among them (1 John 2:18-19).

We last hear of Ephesus in the warnings to the seven churches Rev 2:1-7. While the date of Revelation is disputed, it was probably towards the end of Domitian's reign 81-96. This church is approved for its hard work, perseverance and discernment and endurance. Despite suffering so much they had not grown weary but they had lost their first love – seemingly contradictory. In their favour was the fact that they did not tolerate the work of wicked men, particularly the Nicolaitans. If they did not change, the church was in danger of dying.

Why has Paul's Writing Changed so Much?

The Pastorals are not just more of the same. They cannot be interpreted just as one does the other 10 letters in the Pauline corpus. The critics are correct that there are significant differences. This author believes there were deep fundamental changes that occurred in the Ephesian church and in Paul himself which required a major rethink on Paul's behalf of every aspect of church life and perhaps even doctrinal emphasis. Differences in the circumstances explain many of the changes.

The Changes

Paul had changed. He has spent possibly four years in prison. He has had time to think, something hard to do when you are preaching and working for a living. Perhaps he reconsidered the way he had been organizing the church. He appointed elders that would cause trouble. He was now old and described himself as "Paul the aged" (Phil 1:20,21). With this must have come the realisation that his ministry had to be carried on by others who did not have his training, character, experience or the direct encounter with the Saviour.

The church itself had changed. Paul's thrust had been evangelism and teaching (Acts 20:21) but now there as a well established church with established doctrines. Had the emphasis on teaching and evangelism in a church abuzz with supernatural power led to a lack of depth of character in the believers? Nowhere in I Timothy do we read of Timothy being involved with the miraculous other than needing to stir up the gift within him.

The church was becoming more settled. Was Paul himself aware that the extreme supernatural dynamic was waning and the church had to change with that. God's enemies were no longer struck down but had to be met with other weapons, weapons that all believers could possess – faith and discernment.

There was a major falling away. In 1 Timothy there is a strong emphasis on believers who had fallen away. Presumably this occurred during the 5 years approximately between the farewell to the elders and his return.

1:5-6 - They had substituted meaningless talk for a pure heart, good conscience and sincere faith

1:19-20 - They had not held on to faith and a good conscience

3:6-7 - Church officers were not to be recent converts due to trouble with pride leading to a fall

4:1 - There was a warning about a greater falling away by people following what may be proto-Gnostic teachings

5:15 – Some of the younger widows, through idleness had turned astray

6:9-10 – Love of money had turned the hearts of some

6:21 – Some had fallen because of religious speculation and a claim of superior knowledge.

This emphasis on falling away is not matched in any other book.

While the sins of those who have fallen were obvious, Paul warned Timothy that there are some whose sins are more subtle (5:25). He had probably appointed many of the heretical leaders. Perhaps this was an inkling at the greater falling away that would yet come

Doctrine had changed. Doctrine has changed in the sense that it had been narrowed down into an accepted body or deposit which must be guarded (1 Tim 6:3, 20-21). In an established church there is no longer the necessity to argue and define what Christian teaching was. The ambiguity and ignorance of just twenty years earlier with John the Baptist's disciples does not occur. Heresy could be quickly and easily recognized by its content and associated lifestyle.

Paul most probably has quoted statements of doctrine in other works (e.g. Rom 1:2-4; Phil. 2:5ff Col 1:15ff. Ephesians 5:14 has the appearance of a hymn). In the Pastorals with the five "faithful sayings" (1 Timothy 1:15; 3:1, 4:9; 2 Timothy 2:11) there is a further development. The writer is apparently using forms developed for catechetical purposes and in 1 Timothy 3:16 also appears to be using a Christian hymn (Guthrie 1990, 632).

Paul had seen Rome. Paul was well travelled though the Hellenistic world and had considerable experience with Roman justice and was proud of his Roman citizenship. Throughout Acts, Rome was presented as not being hostile to the gospel. The governor of Cypress believed, and when the Roman legal system is functioning impartially, the judges made favourable decisions for

Christianity. They realised that the faith was not subversive to order and good government throughout the Empire. When there was an extended period of imprisonment in Caesarea it was because justice is being subverted by the desire for a bribe.

Had Paul comprehended the depravity of the capital? Paul had now stood before Nero in the heart of the empire. Had he met such evil, a man who murdered his mother and his wife? Had he comprehended the corruption, wealth, poverty, cruelty and superstition that he would see there? Certainly he would have had some idea as this was not secret. However seeing is different to hearing. Had he comprehended the perilous nature of the church with such an emperor? Certainly the church was going to have to walk a fine line and the opinion that the non-Christians held of the church was going to be very important.

Mounce adds further, "Years of Roman imprisonment, interaction with his guard and the people of the city, could easily have had an effect on both his thought and expression" (2000, lxiii). It is very reasonable to expect that Paul is more intimately acquainted with Latin at this time, explaining the many Latinisms in the Pastorals.

The world was changing. The faith was turning the world upside down and making inroads even into the palace of Caesar. Paul had experienced persecution but the believers had been largely left unscathed. Roman law had protected the Way. This was all going to change soon as violent persecution would soon break out against them. How much did Paul sense that this was imminent? Ephesus at this time had been actively seeking to establish a regional temple to the imperial cult. It had been passed over for Pergamum and

Smyna but a temple was finally dedicated in 88/91 AD. This time it would be to a living emperor who would claim supremacy over Artemis[32].

The attack on the church has changed. The church was first attacked by persecution where a concerted attempt was made to extinguish at least the Hellenistic expression of the faith (Acts 8-9). Paul of all men knew the sincere motives of these persecutors (Acts 26:9-11). Later the church would have to deal with the Jews who believed that Christianity was an "add on" to the law and required the Gentile believers to be converted to Judaism (Acts 15:5). The Council of Jerusalem decided against making Gentiles full Jews through circumcision and the keeping of the Law. But there were moral and dietary requirements put on the gentiles (Acts 19:21) which recognized the sincere views held by the Jews. In Corinth with all its thoughtlessness and extremes, the Christians and its leaders were also sincere. Quite possibly they had incorrectly understood some of Paul's preaching and practices and were competing with themselves to be a better expression of Christ. (1 Cor 1:12). The Corinthian church responded to correction and its own leadership was able to correct the excesses.

The Ephesian attack is fundamentally different as the sincerity of the earlier heretics was missing. Now leaders were leading people astray for the basest of motives, money and the desire to have a following.

---

[32] For more details refer to Imperial Cult in this authors Ephesus – its History and Religious Setting.

The changed nature of the ministry. Paul did not have in mind a short term ministry, of sending an emissary, read a letter for those in error, take up an offering for the poor in Jerusalem and then leave like we see with the Corinthian problem. Paul's intention through Timothy was to build deep roots and strengths in the congregation. The strengths we see built into the Ephesian Church in Revelation were all part of the work that Timothy was commissioned to undertake. The Church was praised in Rev 2.2 for having put false apostles to the test and there is no mention of the heresy encountered in Ignatius's letter to the Ephesians (C. 110 AD) other than they were not deceived 8.1.[33]

Exhortation in Rev 2	As reflected in 1 Timothy
Hard work	Clothing with good deeds 2:10 Train yourself to be Godly 4:7 Work hard in your ministry 4:13-16 Fulfilling family responsibilities 5:3-5 The good work of the widows on the list 5:9-10 The young women not to be idle 5:11-14 Church given to charity 5:16 Slaves are to honour their masters so the faith is not slandered 6:1 The rich are rich in good deeds 6:18
perseverance	Those who have not persevered and wandered Continuing in faith love& holiness The widow who is alone 5:5 Take hold of eternal life 6:12-14 Taking hold of eternal life through good works 6:19
discernment	Not devoting themselves to myths 1:4

---

[33] Of course it could be claimed that this heresy is not mentioned because it is later than these writings (Brown, 1997, 667).

	Choosing your leaders
	Knowing how to conduct yourself in God's household 3:15
	The way to treat other Christians 5:1-2
	Recognizing those elders worthy of double honour 5:17
	Do nothing out of favouritism 5:21
	Hidden good deeds show themselves in the character of the giver 5:25
	False teachers have the wrong motivations 6:3-5
	Godliness and contentment better than wealth 6:6-9
	Trust in God not wealth 6:17
	Turn away from godless chatter 6:20
endurance	Fight the good fight 1:18
	Fight the good fight 6:11
	Guard what has been entrusted to you 6:20
Hating the work of evil men	False teachers coming
	Those who sin to be rebuked publicly 5:20
	Don't share in the sins of others 5:22

Table 2. Comparison of 1 Timothy to Revelation 2.

The church was changing as an institution, going from the early enthusiasm of a group of believers to becoming highly structured. The church had also gone from a period of error held in good faith through to teachers who deliberately lead the members into gross error. People were falling away from the faith while others, who were resolute in the faith, were losing their first love. "Shell shocked" might be a term used to describe them as we last encounter them.

A foundation was being re-established by Timothy, later built on by John, which would leave his church well equipped to recognize the error of the later heretics

The changing nature of discernment. It is said (Dibelius and Conzelmann 1972, 4) that that church order was not Pauline as we know it from the acknowledged Pauline works (Von Campenhausen 1969, 58) or even Acts. This is a reasonable observation. To then demand the pseudographic nature of the book does not recognise the need for a very profound change of direction in church order.

No longer were the witness and leading of the Spirit the acceptable guide for church leadership. Paul's own ministry as an evangelist occurred after he and Barnabas were set aside by the Spirit. We first hear of Paul appointing church officers during the first missionary journey (Acts 14:21-24) where leaders are appointed after a couple of months at the most. What could they really know of these men's suitability when in 1 Timothy there is a warning about a man being able to hide his sins? This method of appointment which was not based on very close scrutiny (Guthrie 1990, 626) and must have involved the discernment of the Spirit was a process that worked at least initially. On Paul's second missionary journey he found the churches prospering. As this practice appeared to work it is not surprising that Paul probably continued using this system.

However, when Paul wrote 1 Timothy, in Ephesus there were men certainly known to Paul and most likely appointed by him[34] who

---

[34] Similarly Fee 1985, 142. Guthrie says that the eldership system in operation

were leading the church astray. The old method had left the founder "burned badly enough" (Fee 1985, 149) when it proved fallible and was now working against the best interest of the church (Guthrie 1990, 627). It was almost as if the saying "what is the witness of the Spirit" has been replaced with "what are the facts." Paul's new strict guidelines, which are virtually all moral and observable, not spiritual (see table below). It was almost as if someone from off the street without the Spirit could say to the church "these men should be your leaders". There is now a group leadership and there is no hint of the prophetic ministry functioning individually (Glassman 1987, 71).

When Paul met the Ephesian Elders on his way to Jerusalem in Acts 20:25, he described the overpowering compulsion driving him as like being "captive to the spirit" (Acts 20:21). Paul doesn't know what will happen to him there but he does know that the elders will never see his face again (20:25). It seems unlikely that the Apostle is simply saying that all the elders will be dead by the time he comes to Ephesus again. The thrust seems to be rather that he will never see Ephesus again and he knows this by the Spirit. Yet probably five years later, he is in the vicinity again and if he has not already visited Ephesus he has had to take definite steps to avoid it. In 1 Tim 3:14 Paul is again planning to visit, contrary to what he knew from the Spirit.

---

in Ephesus in Acts 20 "may have even been suggested by the apostle himself and have been instituted immediately after his departure" (1957, 30). Paul spent two years establishing a church in the city. It would seem remiss that Paul had not established a system of church government. If Apollos who at first taught John's baptism could quickly be an approved and respected evangelist, how much more easily could leaders have been found from the twelve Christians who followed John's baptism that Paul found when he first arrived?

Is it not surprising that his writings changed with less stress on the subjective work of the Spirit inside the person observing. More emphasis is placed on looking at the fruit of good works which reflected the inner work done by the Holy Spirit on the person observed.

The role of the Emperor was changing. Paul wrote at a time when Asia and particularly Ephesus was in a period of transition from the worship of its local gods to a time where the Imperial cult would take prominence. There are three words which have prominence in the Epistles that are not common in acknowledged Pauline epistles, :"saviour", "appearance" and "piety". These words have very strong connection to the Imperial cult and it can even be argued that the letters have a subversive element, This is explored in Chapter 5.

This writer finds the only surprise is in comparing the personal letter of 1 Timothy with books written to churches in totally different times with different ministry problems and techniques and expecting the books to be the same. In such a setting we would be more surprised if Paul's approach was similar to other epistles. The existing leadership could not be counted on and new leaders had to be appointed. The heretics would not respond to arguments of logic and scripture as they had shipwrecked their faith.

3. THE PURPOSE OF EACH LETTER

It would appear unlikely that there was little new information in these epistles as both Timothy and Titus had spent years with Paul and knew his ways well. These matters must have been discussed on many occasions and certainly prior to their departure, Timothy to Ephesus and Titus to Crete. The letters are clearly only semi-personal and intended to buttress the position of Paul's delegates as they went about their tasks of re-organising the church.

The letters of 1&2 Timothy and Titus claim to be written to instruct the recipients how to perform their ministry as apostolic delegates in their assemblies. As they are concerned with the life of the church they are termed "ecclesiological". They have been called the Pastoral Epistles only since the 18th century.

The value of these epistles is the light it sheds on the following subjects:

o   The administration and life of the church. They give clear directions for the qualities of its leaders, how to deal with different age groups and the administration of charity.

o   The value of sound doctrine and how to deal with heretics. It is not enough to be sincere in what you believe.

o   The need for a consecrated life, our actions must match our belief.

○   The value of creeds and catchy sayings as a means of spreading the gospel. No creed but Jesus Christ is out of harmony with the Pastorals.

○   They provide historical information on the close of Paul's life and the development of the church as it approached the close of the first century.

Date

Paul would have reached Rome early in AD 60 and was a prisoner there for two years before his release. The earliest date for 1 Timothy and Titus is AD 62. Tradition states that Paul was executed during the persecution of Nero[35], obviously the latest possible date for 2 Timothy. Eusebius places his death to Nero's 13th year, A.D. 67.[36]

1 Timothy

There have been attempts to see the Pastoral Epistles, with 1 Timothy in particular as a church manual dealing with how to order the church[37]. Groups as diverse as Roman Catholics, Plymouth Brethren and Presbyterians all claim their organisational authority from the Epistles (Fee 1985, 143). While this view is

---

[35]Emperor of Rome who murdered his own mother and wife. When two thirds of Rome burned in 64, to divert attention from himself, Nero blamed the Christians. The first official persecution followed and was very savage.

[36] Eusebius, Hist Eccl 2.25.7

[37] For an outline of 1 Timothy as a church manual see Fee 1985, 143.

popular and entrenched (Fee 1985, 143), it is unsatisfactory because the epistles leave more questions than they answer. Fee observes that this confusion is brought about by what he sees as the ad hoc[38] nature of the epistles and if it is ad hoc then church order was not the primary reason for writing (1985, 143).

Instead of setting the church in order the writer of 1 Timothy instead gives two seemingly different reasons for the letter. The reason frequently given for writing is found in 1 Timothy 3:14-15:

[14] I hope to come to you soon, but I am writing these instructions to you so that, [15] if I am delayed, you may know how one ought to behave in the household of God, which is the church of the living God, the pillar and bulwark of the truth.

This passage says that there is appropriate behaviour for those who believe in the living God and that Timothy needs to know what that is. Paul will elaborate through the book how important it is for those outside the church to have the right opinion of the faith as seen by the conduct of the believers e.g. 1 Timothy 5:14. The second reason in 1 Timothy 1:3 appears very different: to protect the faith of the believers.

[3] I urge you, as I did when I was on my way to Macedonia, to remain in Ephesus so that you may instruct certain people not to teach any different doctrine,

---

[38] By "ad hoc" we cannot say "thrown together" as it will be shown that the rhetorical features of this letter are very sophisticated (Gill 2008, 110)

The need to refute error and instructions on how to lead Christian lives were not mutually exclusive. We will attempt to show that this is cause and symptom of the Ephesian heresy. Ephesus was the centre for evangelism of the whole region so it was essential that the heresy be stamped out here as it would otherwise permeate through the whole of Asia Minor.

In Ephesus Paul found Judaistic teachers, not the legalists of 10 years previously, but a combination of the worst elements of current Rabbinical Hermeneutics and libertine elements that may have later developed into Gnosticism, 1 Tim 1:4, 4:7 4:3, 2 Tim 2:18.   These teachers made it necessary for Paul to lay down plain rules concerning church worship.   Specifically he writes to:

(i). Bolster Timothy's spirits: It would have been difficult for a man with any feelings of inferiority to deal with men with a superiority complex. He reminds him of the gifts he has received. 1 Tim 4:14, 6:12, 6:20.

(ii). Impart guidance concerning the doctrines that were destroying the church in Ephesus. The false teachers were exposed and stress is laid on choosing the right kind of (replacement) leaders and correcting them if they go astray.

(iii). Directions for proper conduct during public worship.

Because of the problems with the leadership there was little point in writing to the church as he normally did. They did after all know Paul's teaching and no amount of teaching will correct men who refuse to follow it.

Titus

There are a number of similarities between 1 Timothy and Titus:

- o Style and vocabulary are similar
- o There is a concern for proper church government
- o The opponents seem similar
- o There is a charge to rebuke heretics
- o Both men are outside of normal church structures
- o They are private, not church correspondence
- o They both address specific situations (Mounce 2000, lx)

But there are also differences:

- o The opponents were less of a concern in Titus
- o Titus was mainly teaching for new believers
- o The elders were not rebuked as they are not yet appointed
- o There is not the same urgency in Crete as in Ephesus
- o Crete's problems arose from outside the church (aberrant Judaism and Cretian culture). (Mounce 2000, lxi).

Titus may well have been written before 1 Timothy[39], though there was probably not a long gap between them.

There were Cretans at the day of Pentecost (Acts 2:11) and a church may have already been established by the time Paul and Titus visited in events after Acts 28. Paul may have spent a considerable time in Crete. Churches were established in a number of cities (1:5) and their leaders had been in the faith long enough to have believing children (1:6). There was time enough for opponents to start to arise (1:11).

The reputation of Cretans was not good and apparently well deserved. The Christians there needed a thorough sanctification. Elders must be blameless and those who could not control their tongues were to be silenced. Specifically he writes to:

(i). Urge Titus to come to Nicopolis, 3:12 and care for the church in the meanwhile.

(ii). Speed on their way Zenas and Apollos, 3:12

(iii) Give directions for the promoting of sanctification. It is a good summary of Christian doctrine.

From his descriptions of the residents of Crete, Paul must have considered the task given to Titus to be more difficult than that given to Timothy.

---

[39] The ordering of Paul's letters have more to do with length than order of writing (Mounce 2000, lxi)

2 Timothy

The mood had changed. Paul had been arrested, possibly at or on his way to Miletus (Mounce 2000, lxii) and taken to Rome. Possibly the arrest was instigated by Alexander as a reprisal for Paul excommunicating him (1 Tim. 1:20, c.f. 2 Tim. 4:14) (Mounce 2000, lxii). Timothy was most likely still in Ephesus as he was aware of the situation in Asia (2 Tim. 1:15). The heresy addressed was very similar to that in 1Timothy. The conditions of his imprisonment were much harsher suggested by the need for a warm coat and Luke, although a friend, may have been needed in his role as Physician. Paul was feeling the effects of being deserted by almost every one (2 Tim. 4:9). Despite his first hearing going well Paul knew he will die soon.

While there is a common literary style, the content of 2 Timothy is very different than the other two Pastorals. The letter is highly personal and full of encouragement and personal remembrances. There are only two references to false teachers (2 Tim. 2:14-18, 2:23-3:9). Specifically he writes to:

(i). Urge Timothy to come to Rome, (2 Tim. 4:9-13)

(ii). To urge him to cling to and depend on sound doctrine, He warns of a great coming apostasy, (2 Tim. 3:1-9)

Personal Sketches

Timothy

Timothy was the son of a Gentile father and his name meant "honouring or worshipping god". His mother was a Jewess who was also a believer. Timothy had been instructed in the scriptures from birth by his mother (and grandmother?) (2 Tim 3:15, 1:5). His mother's marriage to a Gentile would have been viewed as illegitimate by both the Jews and the Christians, but far from being a bastard he would become Paul's true son, (1 Tim 1:2). Despite being an illegitimate marriage (from a Jewish perspective), Timothy would still be considered a Jew.

He joined Paul and Silas at Lystra on the second missionary journey, probably as a successor to the "quitter," John Mark. He was already a highly esteemed Christian, Acts 16:2, most likely converted by Paul on, or as a consequence of, his first missionary journey. Because of this and his close relationship Paul has no hesitation referring to him as his child, 1 Cor 4:17, 1 Tim 1:2, 2 Tim 1:2. Timothy collaborated with Paul in six of his remaining letters, 1 and 2 Thessalonians 2 Corinthians, Colossians, Philemon, Philippians cf. Rom. 16:2.

Timothy was commissioned for his task by the laying on of hands and prophesy, 1 Tim 1:18, 4:14, 2 Tim 1:6. Paul had Timothy circumcised (presumably his Gentile father had previously objected) so there would be no hindrance in his witnessing to the Jews. Eventually he was to be imprisoned for a time in Rome Heb 13:23 possibly after returning there to Paul.

His Personality

He was amiable, Phil 2:19-22, V20 "I have no one like him who takes a genuine interest in your welfare."

He was faithful, Paul knew he could count on him, 1 Tim 4:12; 2 Tim 4:11, 1 Cor 4:17. This picture we can have of Timothy puts emphasis on: :

- o His natural timidity, 1 Cor 16:10&11; 2 Tim 1:7

- o His youth, 1 Tim 4:12; 2 Tim 2:22

- o Frequent ailments, 1 Tim 5:23. This would not encourage travel which was perilous at best.

- o Being a little negligent, needing to stir up the gifts in him, 1 Tim 4:12-16; 2 Tim 1:6, 3:14ff

But this image of Timothy is totally in keeping with the New Testament record. While perhaps there was some timidity it cannot have been excessive as he had carried out, and probably alone, missions for Paul to Thessalonica and Corinth. The exhortations to boldness may have more to do with the strength of the opposition (Fee 1995, 2) and their quarrelsome nature. Timothy was not young by our modern standards as he would be at least over 30 at this stage[40]. Kelly describes him as "an almost

---

[40] The reference to Timothy's youth does not require us to find an earlier date for the Pastorals. Paul himself is referred to as a young man Acts 7:58 when he was at least 30.

reluctant successor (to Paul) whose weaknesses are as apparent as his virtues" (Kelly 1981, 4-5).

Titus

He was a Gentile by birth and probably a convert of Paul. Though he is not mentioned at all in Acts, he is first implied in 15:2 c.f. Galatians 2:1&3, where he was taken along to the Council of Jerusalem with Paul and Barnabas. There the matter of circumcising Gentiles was resolved. Titus was the test case as the Judaisers would have demanded his circumcision, Gal 2:3. His life must have been exemplary and his importance in the churches' progress cannot be underestimated. Previously he had resolved the Corinthian problem which was very delicate[41] and took up the offering for Jerusalem (2 Cor. 8:16:24). "He breathed the spirit of Paul" (Henrickson 1983, 39).

Tradition says he became the first Bishop of Crete after the islands initial evangelisation by Paul.

A Comparison of the Two

Titus would most likely have been the older of the pair, (c.f. 1 Tim 4:12 and Titus 2:15). Where Timothy needed prodding, (1 Tim 1:6), Titus goes forward on his own (2 Cor 8:16-17). With the

---

[41]This crisis was caused when the church in Corinth would not remove an extremely sinful man and rejected Paul's apostolic authority.

handling of the Corinthian problem Titus is shown to be the stronger character and more competent. Despite this, Timothy seems to be the person Paul would rather have around. No one else is mentioned as often as being his companion. When Paul faces death Timothy is the one who is called for.

Paul

"A definite change took place after the imprisonment of Paul. The man himself was different, for although he was unready to quit the ardent pursuit of his calling, as Philippians showed (Phil. 3:12), time was against him. In Philemon he described himself as "Paul the aged" (Philemon 9), and in Philippians he indicated that death might not be far distant (Phil 1:20-21). He was relying increasingly upon the aid of his younger associates, who were still free and better able than he to carry on the work of preaching" (Tenny 1973, 331).

A Warning for Today from the Pastorals

We know little about the founding of the Church in Crete but Acts does contain the details of the founding of Ephesus. Apart from a brief transit stop, Paul did not reach Ephesus until his third missionary journey, arriving there c. 53, and ministered in the city for about two years (Acts 19:10). While there, many notable miracles were performed and so many converts were made that the artisans who made shrines to Artemis[42] caused a riot because their

---

[42]She was also called Diana. Her temple in Ephesus, one of the Seven Wonders

livelihood was being affected (Acts 19:23-40).

Following the riot, Paul left Ephesus, travelling through Greece and Macedonia, collecting money for the impoverished Jerusalem church, arriving back in Asia Minor a few months afterwards. As he travelled to Antioch, the Ephesian elders met at Miletus. Paul gave them his final instructions. Tragically, this very young church was warned that from out of the midst of their eldership would rise destructive heretics (Acts 20:29-30). Already the seed for the church's possible destruction had been planted, despite its being founded by the great Apostle, Paul.

Paul felt an overpowering need to preach the Gospel where it had never been preached before (Rom 15:20), and had a strong desire to go to Spain (Rom 15:24), but only after completing his mission to Jerusalem. Despite years of imprisonment in Caesarea and Rome, he probably reached Spain. Now, instead of planting new churches, his most trusted and capable men must go to the established churches and repair the damage that had been done and to appoint new elders.

His practice in the past had been to appoint elders soon after a church was founded (Acts 14:21-23), often out of necessity, but his new advice was to change all this - no longer were new converts to be made elders.

Had the heresy been a low level intrusion, we would hardly have

of the World, was the most sacred in the eastern Mediterranean.

expected this strong stand, but it must have struck at the very heart and continuance of the church. It remains a solemn lesson how a church with the best of leadership and heritage can so quickly self-destruct. Pastors must remain eternally vigilant of the charges given to them by God.

4. THE EPHESIAN HERESY

The seed of the heresy was already sown by the time Paul wrote his Epistle to the Ephesians where he addressed most of the false practices found in the Pastorals[43]. The polarisation in the church was appearing to begin (Payne 1981, 187) but it was not given any where near the prominence it is in the Pastorals. About one-third (Gritz 1991, 106) of 1 Timothy deals with a heresy that troubled Ephesus. Paul uses medical terms to compare his healthy doctrine with that of the heretics. The gospel is "sound words" (1 Tim 6:3) or "healthy teaching" (Fee 1985, 144) whereas the heretics are "depraved in mind" (1 Tim. 6:5) with a morbid craving for controversy (1 Tim. 6:4) (Fee 1985, 144).

The effect of the heresy in the First City of Asia is obvious. However little is known about neither what the heresy actually was nor the argument needed to refute it. It simply does not fit easily with any of the known heresies. Yet Timothy's presence in Ephesus was the measure of how dangerous Paul considered the threat to that church that could eat away at it like gangrene (1 Tim 2:17, Mounce 2000, lxxv). It is even questionable if it should even be called a heresy as it does not appear to be "a well-thought-out cohesive system" (Mounce 2000, lxxv). Paul does not argue with the heretics, the truth is a deposit which is taken for granted. His 'argument" is to reminds them of what they already know to be true, a rhetorical approach termed "paraenesis". After all, how can anyone formulate a reasoned argument "against empty chatter and quarrels about words" (Mounce 2000, lxxv). Despite this difficulty, what we make of this heresy will determine how we

---

43 Payne lists these as False teaching, Eph 3:14; 4:14; 5:6-7, Controversies 2:14-15; 4:2-6, 13-16, 25, 29-32; 5:6-7, 21, meaningless talk 4:14, 29-31; 5:4,6, Judiasers 2:14-15, Antinomianism 2:1-3; 4:17; 5:3-7, 21 (1981, 187).

interpret the book.

At the core of this heresy were six errors.

- o The heretics taught for financial reward 1 Tim 6:5; Tit 1:11

- o They deceived 2 Tim 3:13

- o They were hypocrites 2 Tim 3:5; Tit 1:16, 3:8-9

- o They argued over words not substance 1 Tim 1:4, 6; 4:2; 2 Tim 2:14, 16, 23; Tit 1:10; 3:9

- o There is a list of vices 1 Tim 1:9-10; 2 Tim 3:2-4

- o They had success among women 2 Tim 3:6 (Young 1994, 15)

This structure has been identified by many (e.g. Young 1994, 20) as an argument of the philosophers against opposing teachers that was common between the period from 70 AD to the end of the second century[44] (Karris 1973, 552-54). Examples are given in Table 3

---

44 Karris is correct in identifying the current philosophical and rhetorical pattern but goes too far when he argues that this form is only intended to separate the two parties and does bear on the real problems occurring in Ephesus (Mounce 2000, lxxv, Karris 1973, 563-4).

Person	Reason for use
Plato	Against the Sophists
Philo	To establish the soundness of Judaism
Dio Chysostom	Against the Cynics
Lucian	Against the wandering Cynics
Tatian & Athenagoras	To establish Christianity as the true philosophy and fostered good morals

Table 3. Common nature of the core of the heresy. (Young 1994, 15, see also Karris 1973, 555&6)

This argument had three benefits

- o It "produced aversion for the opponents and sympathy for the writer's position" (Young 1994, 16)

- o The writer's teaching was not linked to that of the heretics.

- o It showed "who had the right to and actually did impart genuine wisdom and truth" (Karris 1973, 556).

The Pastorals differ from this arrangement in that Paul does not need to convince Timothy of his credentials.   The strong connection between the Pastorals and Socratic letters[45] suggests

---

[45] The so-called Socratic Letters, date from the first century AD and are thought to be mostly spurious. The connection has been detailed by Benjamin Fiore where he shows 12 similarities between two traditions "hortatory instructions addressed to young officials on the conduct and attitudes expected of them and their constituencies" and "epistolary exhortations to a way of life consistent with the traditions of a philosophical school" (Fiore 1986 232 quoted Young 1994,

that the writer was acquainted with rhetorical theory (Young 1994, 19). This rhetorical pattern may have been the source of some of the specific language used (Mounce 2000, lxxvi). It suggests that for his opponents, who seemed to value the argument more than the facts, "were more rhetoricians than they were theologians" (Mounce 2000, lxxiii).

This six point argument may be ancient but the modern reader may have little trouble putting modern names to it. In this sense there is almost universality to this heresy which will make the Pastorals relevant in dealing with a wide variety of aberrant Christian behaviour, almost a manual for discipleship and a paradigm for dealing with heresy.[46]

Those who hold to pseudonymous authorship would see this modelling of character of the heretics around accepted formula as evidence that we are looking at a fictional paradigm – one that encompasses as broad a group as possible (Dibelius and Conzelmann, 1972, 66). However, the use of conventional rhetorical features does not prove that Paul was not the author and he was not addressing a true situation.

Despite the timelessness at the core of the heresy, if Pauline authorship is accepted then there was a specific aberration related to specific people (2 Tim 2:17, 4:14) that required urgent and immediate attention, just as it did in Corinth. Aspects of the heresy that go beyond the stock charges of the philosophers are:

---

19)

[46] Some would argue from this general nature that the heresy is in fact just a literary construct and attempts to reconstruct the heresy as misguided (Young 1994, 20)

- o Endless genealogies (1 Tim. 1:4; Tit 3:9)

- o Teaching the Law (1 Tim. 1:7)

- o Forbidding marriage and abstaining from certain foods (1 Tim 4:3)

- o The resurrection is past 2 Tim 2:18

- o The Jewish nature of the heretics Tit 1:10-16

- o Arguing over the Law Tit 3:9 (Young 1994, 16)

Paul deals primarily with the loose living and contentious character of the heretics[47]. They are dealt with in the letters only as a contrast to how Timothy and other readers should act. The link between godlessness and immorality is expounded in Romans 1. Timothy in this sense serves as an "ideal Christian teacher" (Young 1994, 16). The heresy is a present danger. He had warned the church about the coming troubles Acts 20:29 and there he called the heretics "savage wolves". Paul's own role when he as an apostle of the law is very similar in effect, yet he was to find grace. The heretics were to lose that grace, shipwrecking their faith (1 Tim 1:19). Paul, in 2 Timothy 3 likens the heretics in their midst to the spirit that will permeate the church at the end of the age.

[3]lovers of themselves, lovers of money, boasters, arrogant, abusive, disobedient to their parents, ungrateful, unholy, inhuman, implacable, slanderers, profligates, brutes, haters of good, [4]treacherous, reckless, swollen with conceit, lovers of pleasure rather than lovers of God, [5]holding to the outward form of

---

[47] Refer to the two fold purpose for writing the epistle.

godliness but denying its power. Avoid them!. See also 1 Tim. 6:4-5, 9-10.

The orientation of these heretics has moved from centring around Christ to now revolving around themselves. Duty to man and God has disappeared (Lock 1978, 105) . In their attempt to liberate themselves they simply replaced the Lordship of Christ for that of Satan (1 Tim. 1:20, 5:15). The question to be answered is whether the heresy led to the conduct or whether the conduct led to the heresy (Geitz 1991, 109-10). The latter seems to be the thrust in verses such as "For the love of money is a root of all kinds of evil, and in their eagerness to be rich some have wandered away from the faith" (1 Tim. 6:10). The stress given to behaviour would suggest that self orientation in the Ephesian Christian was the main problem. Their faith was now no more than a means to feed their greed through financial gain (Titus 1.1). In this they were no better than the silversmiths of the Artemis cult (Acts 19:23-41). By contrast the elders and deacons Timothy appointed were to be free of financial gain in their ministry.

It is difficult to know how serious the heresy i.e. the incorrect belief, as opposed to the incorrect behaviour actually was. Guthrie (1990, 628) says its danger was "not so much in falseness as its irrelevance". The doctrine was not Christian but we are struck more with its futility than its error so much so that Paul only denounced it and did not bother to refute it (Guthrie 1990, 628-9). Timothy and Titus as experienced Christian workers were more than capable of that (Guthrie 1990, 629). Their teachings were foolish controversies based on no more than speculations over myths and genealogies. Their disputes about the Law were useless (2 Tim.2:14), unprofitable and worthless (Titus 3:9). This heresy was not the misguided imagination of ill informed teachers but the doctrine of demons (1 Tim 4:1) and so was insidious. This danger of this heresy could be seen in its outworking of strife (Titus 3:9)the way it caused quarrels (2 Tim. 2:23) and ultimately leading to ruin (2 Tim. 2:14). The Pauline virtues of faith, hope and love are in short supply in the arrogant (2 Tim. 3:2) argumentative and divisive (Titus 1:11, 3:9-11) false teachers.

There was a radical truth at the core of the Gospel which was seized upon by the heretics and was resulting in the disruption of the normal social structure in the home and church. Mappes describes this saying "slaves disobeyed masters, women usurped the role of men, in the church as women were emancipated from the traditional domination of their husbands, and widows became attracted to an aesthetic lifestyle" (1999, 459). The message of emancipation was at least implicit in Paul's teaching as he had advised slaves to gain their freedom if they could (1 Cor. 7:21) and encouraged women to be taught the faith (1Tim. 2:11). This message of emancipation must have received a welcome among the oppressed as they reflected on the implications of Paul's teaching. The equality of men and woman before God could not allow the continuation of the cultural subjection of women to a life of servitude, repression and ignorance. Emancipation is more than implicit; it is at the core of the Gospel. It has been the outworking of the Gospel as it permeates society. Unfortunately it was a truth held without balance and without the moral character and wisdom of its leaders to guide it.

This is not a gradual outworking they were seeking but a revolution. The resurrection was passed and this was a time of reigning with Christ, suffering had passed (Mappes 1999, 458).

Such a radical expression of Christianity would have made the church a pariah in the Ephesian society. Over time, the ultimate outworking of emancipation would have been the attempted removal of the final shackle, political chains of Rome. The events of the Jewish revolt would demonstrate how perilous that would have been for the church. Salvation in the Pastorals is a past (2 Tim. 1:9; Titus 3:5), present (1 Tim. 1:15; 4:8) and future (1 Tim. 4:8,16; 2 Tim. 4:18) event. For the heretics who believed the resurrection had passed it was only a past and present event. Perhaps the difference between freedom and salvation had been blurred. There is an association but freedom needs an understanding of its nature otherwise it can develop into a parody of that very liberation which would lead to another form of slavery (Spencer 1974, 220).

A church that was settling in to a delay before Christ's re-appearing had time to change society and had time to set its priorities. Paul prevented the Ephesian church from moving in the radical direction of the heretics and could have found it expedient to have backed back on the role of women (Similarly Spencer 1994, 220). But with Paul there should not have been a gap between theory and practice and he strongly criticised Peter for discriminating between Jew and Gentile (Gal. 2:11-14) (Spencer 1974, 220). What would Paul do in a modern church which discriminates between men and women?

Some of those that were taking the church into error were its own leaders (Acts 20:30, 1 Tim. 1:3, 7; 6:3). This is different from Galatia and Corinth where the problems were caused by outsiders (Gal. 2.4; cf 2 Cor. 11:4). The danger of these teachers was the greater because of their association with Paul, so giving them credibility (Acts 20:13-31) . It is expected that at this stage the church in Ephesus was based on home churches each presumably with at least one elder. The impact on the Ephesian church would not be so much a matter of splitting a congregation into two groups but instead, complete home churches would have departed. The family provided the model for church leadership and so any threat to the household was a threat to the institution (Young 1994, 39)

The authenticity of these epistles as noted is hotly disputed. Those who do not recognize Pauline authorship see here a reference to full blown Gnosticism or even just a general warning about heresy (Young 1994, 3) The heresies suggested fall into four groups, "Jewish, Gnostic, Jewish Gnostic and others ('Proto-Montanists', 'Cerinthians', or 'Marcionites influenced by Valentinianism')" (Young 1994,4-5 try to find Gunther 1973) Gunther's analysis of the different views shows the prevailing, but contested view is that the heresy came from a Jewish Gnostic setting. They were he claims believers whose background was a mystic-apocalyptic, ascetic, non conformist syncretistic Judaism more akin to Essenism than to other well-known 'school' or holiness sect (Gunther 1973, 315 Quoted young 1994.3) This lack of consensus among scholars gives rise to even more theories (Young 1994, 3).

Marcion

The heretic Marcion C.140 wrote a book called Antitheses, a word found in 1 Timothy 6:60. A late date for the Pastorals would allow for the works to be a direct attack on Marcion. An attack on Marcion is seen by some in the claim that the Law is good (1 Tim 1:8) as Marcion totally rejected the Old Testament (Guthrie 1990, 610). Knosis was a word Marcion used to describe his writings while in Timothy 6:20 we read of "the opposing ideas of what is falsely called knowledge" (Guthrie 1990, 610). The acceptance of Pauline authorship would make the theory of directly countering Marcion impossible.

The dependence of the Pastorals on Marcion is not given much credence now. Dibelius and Conzelmann maintain that his teaching cannot be seen in the heresy Paul attacks (1972, 2). Marcion had Gnostic tendencies but was not a Gnostic (Bruce 1992, 251) nor was he a teacher of the Law (Mounce 2000, lxx).

Gnostic Theory

Gnosticism when fully developed was a heresy which was to plague the second century church and, it is often said, is still attacking the church in its different forms today.[48] Guthrie believes "the alignment of the Pastorals with second century Gnosticism might never have occurred had it not been for the need to postulate satisfactory motives for the author when the Pauline origin had been denied (1990, 629-30). It is disputed whether this heresy actually existed[49] in the first century and scholars generally refer to proto-gnosticism during this period (Arnold 1989, 7). Far from being a unified system it was a speculative religious belief with its teachers taking as they chose from Platonic philosophy, oriental mysticism, cabbalistic Judaism and Christianity.

---

[48] E.g. Kendal, R.T. *Westminster Record* Oct 1984, 3 "Gnosticism is alive and well today. It is not called that, we know it as Liberal Christianity, Modernism, where the infallibility of scripture is denied and by and large is the theological system that undergird the modern ecumenical movement"

[49] Arnold is adamant that no evidence exists for the existence of Gnosticism in first centaury Asia Minor (1989, 8)

Gnosticism took many varied forms, from gross immorality to a highly ethical life. This great variation has made it difficult to come to agreement on what Gnosticism even is. Gnostics were united in their rejection of the incarnation of Christ and their attempt to come to God by their own reasoning.

The name comes from the Greek *Ginosko* - to know or understand. Gnosticism's core was the "mystery religions" which mediate secret knowledge leading to salvation and from magic whose knowledge confers supernatural powers and union with God (Bultmann 1964, 692-3). This was nothing new to the Ephesians as there were mysteries associated with the worship of Artemis. Gnosticism was set in the framework of contemporary philosophy, mythology and astrology and later Christianity. The Gnostics were concerned with ultimate salvation and differed from magic which was about systematizing, understanding and manipulating the supernatural for present benefit (Arnold, 1989, 11).

Because of Gnostic tendencies that existed in the first century, a limited agreement has developed between those who accept and those who deny Pauline authorship (Towner 1987, 96). The heresy itself is said to be, if not full blown Gnosticism, at least an early form of Gnosticism originating in Christians with a Hellenistic Jewish background who merged the associated beliefs into orthodox Christianity (Kelly 1963, 163-4). It may well have developed into full blown Gnosticism at a later time. There are also close similarities with the Hellenistic Judaism found in Colossae (Col. 2:3-8, 16-23).

Matter was seen as inherently evil and some in Ephesus were

teaching a form of aestheticism where marriage was forbidden. Under the influence of Gnostic teaching that marriage would hinder spiritual growth, families would be placed under great stress if one party withdrew from the marriage. The distaste for the material could also explain the aesthetic practices in Ephesus (Towner 1987, 96). It seems that women were most likely to succumb "For among them are those who make their way into households and captivate silly women, overwhelmed by their sins and swayed by all kinds of desires, who are always being instructed and can never arrive at a knowledge of the truth" (2 Tim. 3:6-7)

Gnosticism taught God was entirely separate from the creation and so contact was made through a series of intermediary beings (Guthrie, 1990, 617). The soul however was pure celestial element imprisoned by some tragic fate in a material body. Paul had to remind the church that marriage and food were created by God and were to be received with thankfulness (1 Tim 4:3-5). [4]For everything created by God is good, and nothing is to be rejected, provided it is received with thanksgiving; [5]for it is sanctified by God's word and by prayer.

Paul goes out of his way to emphasise the goodness of all God's creation (4:3-5). The heretics spiritualised the resurrection, (2 Tim. 2:18) and boasted a higher knowledge, (1 Tim. 4:2) which Paul said was not real knowledge at all (1 Tim. 4:4). The Jewish flavour of the heresy is shown in that its practitioners were "teachers of the Law" (1 Tim. 1:7) and taken up with fables and genealogies, (1 Tim. 1:4; Titus 1:14). They promoted the renunciation of marriage, abstinence from some foods and possibly from wine. The ability of the latter Gnostics to distort the Old

Testament is shown by Irenaeus in Against Heresies. "Cain and those like him, the men of Sodom and the Egyptians and other such and, in general, all the nations which walked in all kinds of wickedness were saved by the Lord when He descended into the lower regions and came running to Him and received Him into their realm; but Abraham with all the prophets and those who were pleasing to God did not share in this salvation which the serpent who was in Marcion preached"[50] To be sure the heresy was not as extreme at this stage. Its distortion of scripture was not as extreme. Had the heresy been fully developed Paul would have been expected to have written a detailed refutation just as Tertulian did when he encountered it.

The similarity of the terms "was to bring the Christian message into some analogy with heathen Gnosticism and expose it to the acute danger of penetration not merely by Gnostic terminology but by Gnostic problems and conceptions".[51]

Christian knowledge Compared to that of the Gnostics

(i). The knowledge of God is not a theoretical speculation which allows one to live as he pleases

(ii). It is not a mystical relationship, but finds expression in brotherly love

---

[50]

[51]Van Groningen, Gerard. First Century Gnosticism: Its Origin and Motifs (Leiden: E.J. Brill, 1967)183-4.

(iii). It does not arise from within man, but is grounded in God's knowledge of man.

While the proto-Gnostic influence appears strong, the heretics also appear to be Jewish Christians (Young 1994 23).

Jewish Christian Connection

The emphasis between seeing a Gnosticising element or a Judaising influence swings like a pendulum (Towner 1987, 97). The teachers were either Jewish or sympathisers. There are specific references to this influence which include; teachers of the law (1 Tim.1:7), those of the circumcision (Titus 1:10), disputes over the law (Titus 1:14), disputes over the law (Titus 3:9). As well there are references that could be Jewish; myths and genealogies[52] (1 Tim. 1:4), the meaning of *gnosos* (1 Tim. 6:20), the doctrine of the resurrection (2 Tim. 2:18) and ascetic practices (1 Tim. 4:3). This Jewish influence has a restrictive influence affecting lifestyle such as abstinence from certain foods and salvation. The prohibition on marriage could also be associated with aesthetic elements in Judaism. The minimising of faith (1 Tim. 1:5; 2:1-7) and God's mercy (1 Tim. 1:8-11) is an expected outcome of this emphasis. Paul's reminder that God desires that all people be saved (1 Tim. 2:4) may also be countering a Jewish influence. Mounce speculates on the basis of known itinerant Jewish exorcists (Acts 19:13) that there may have been a magical element to his aberration (Mounce 2000, lxx).

---

[52] Possibly haggadic Midrash, allegorical reinterpretation of the Old Testament with imaginative explanations of the genealogies (Mounce 2000, lxx).

The heretics wanted to be teachers of the Law (1 Tim. 1:7), but their minds were deceived by demons (1 Tim. 4:1-2). They could only raise to a speculative use of the Old Testament through their use of Jewish myths and genealogies (1 Tim. 1:4, Titus 1:14). It has been suggested (Ford 1971, 339-40 quoted Young 1994, 25) that the heresy encountered in the Pastorals was "Proto-Montaism". Montanism (arising C156), a Jewish Christian heresy is named after Montanus, who worked in conjunction with two prophetesses Maximilla and Priscilla. They "were accused of paying heed to deceitful spirits and the doctrines of demons. That they dissolved marriages, and that they abstained from wine, introduced new fasts, and abstained from certain foods." (Ford 1971, 339-40 quoted Young 1994, 25) This is exactly the setting of 1 Tim 4:1-5

Instead of works Paul stresses in reply salvation, where salvation is not earned (Titus 3:4-7; 2 Tim. 1:9-10). The teaching of Jesus and Peter is reflected by the understanding of the goodness of creation which supersedes the food laws (Mark 7:1-4; Acts 10:9-16; c.f. Luke 11:40-41; 1 Cor 8-10; Rom. 14). In his response to this Jewish elements Paul does not attack Judaism but makes reference to the core precepts of their faith through the Decalogue (1 Tim. 1:9-10)[53] and the Shema (1 Tim. 2:5). Paul's view was that Christianity is not contrary to true Judaism, only the myths of the heretics.

It is not likely that they represented mainstream Pharisaic Judaism (except perhaps Titus 1:10) as there is no mention of circumcision (Mounce 2000, lxx). The liberty women were experiencing to

---

[53] Refer to the table in the comment on 1 Tim 1:8-11.

learn would certainly not be countenanced under Judaism. While there clearly are aspects that can be called Jewish there are others that seem to be something else (Towner 1987, 103). Their deviation from the true teaching of the Law is so obvious to Paul that he uses the vice list in 1 Tim 1:9-10 that describes them parallels the Decalogue.

Hellenistic Elements

Some of what is thought to be Gnostic thought, such as the denial of the resurrection, could equally be Hellenistic thought (Mounce 2000, lxxi). It could also be the aberration of Christianity we see in Corinth. There was also a similarity between Gnosticism and some streams of Judaism with asceticism and dualism. (Mounce 2000, lxxi). Myths and genealogies can be Gnostic as they tought myths about the families of Aeons separating god from man (Tertullian Adv. Valent.3; De praescr. 33; Irenaeus Adv. Haer. Praef) The same expression could be applied to the Greek mythological heroes (Polybius 9.2.1) and even to the allegorical interpretation of the Old Testament genealogies.

Magic was a very important part of Greek life in Ephesus[54] and the early Christians had not initially separated from it. They kept their magic texts up to the point of the public burning of them (Acts 19:19). Mounce maintains that much of the Pastoral Epistles is aimed as setting the boundary between true religion and superstition (Mounce 2000, lxxi). The opponents are likened to the Egyptian magicians, Jannes and Jambres[55] who argued with Moses

---

[54] Refer to Magic in my Ephesus – Its History and Religious Setting.

[55] By the time of the early church these magicians seem to have developed a reputation as outstanding magicians. Refer Dibelius and Conzelmannn 1972, 117 for references.

(2 Tim. 3:8 c.f. Ex. 7:8ff) and women also may have been involved in magic (1 Tim. 5:3).

Paul had to deal with religious syncretism and Judaism not only in Ephesus but also in Corinth and Colosse (Col. 2:3-8; 1 Cor. 15:12; 1 Cor. 7:1-7; Col. 2:16-23; Col. 2:16, 21) (Mounce 2000, lxxi)

.

Denial of the resurrection

They apparently rejected a future resurrection of the body arguing for a spiritual resurrection that had already passed (2 Tim. 2:18). It is suggested that the heretics may have been attempting to live in the paradise before the fall (Mounce 2000, lxxii) which explains the reference to Gen 1 and 2. This theory would explain vegetarianism and abstinence from marriage.

The Spirit

There is a strong emphasis in the Pastorals on teaching which must be correct and based on the tradition of teaching. There is an office of teacher, which goes against the Gnostic concept of enthusiasm and the free pneuma (Young 1994, 13)

The apocryphal Acts of Paul, is believed to be oral stories about Paul which were later written down when it was claimed there was an environment where many were making claims for his legacy (Young 1994, 24).

Corinthian Connection

The difficulty in finding a coherent heresy may simply be that the heresy itself may not have been based in Christological error nor even a return to Jewish practices (Towner 1987, 112). There are also strong similarities with the heresies Paul wrote against in both Corinth and Ephesus. He attacked in both an over realised eschatology where it was believed that the resurrection was past (1 Cor. 15:12) which resulted in the rejection of marriage (1 Cor. 7 1:7) and aesthetic practices (1 C0r 6:19-20). Salvation was either completed or nearly so and there was no reason to look forward to the eschaton (Towner 1987, 112). While we do not know a great deal about the Ephesian heresy, we do know considerably more about the heresy in Corinth. With regular and easy commerce between the two cities it is reasonable to assume that there was cross fertilisation of ideas.

The enthusiasm that plagued Corinth has been linked to "the speculations of Hellenistic Judaism in which *sophia* and *gnosis* played prominent roles" (Towner 1987, 99). These words are closely associated with the full blown heresy so what is seen in Corinth is sometimes called proto-Gnostic, a vague term. But there is a danger in reading back something from a later time that was foreign in an earlier situation. The Gnostic connection does not adequately address the issue of realised eschatology which had a pervasive effect on the community.

The over-realised eschatology of Corinth may have arisen from a misinterpretation of Paul's teaching that believers have been raised with him and will share in his reign (Rom. 6:3-8, Eph. 2:5, Col. 2:12, c.f. 2 Tim. 2:12). This over-realised eschatology saw believers expecting in this age much if not all of what was to be anticipated in the next. Rather than seeing salvation as a process, the enthusiasts thought they had already experienced the transformation that was to come. This belief led to the strange behaviour we see pictured in the city.

The step from "realised eschatology to emancipatory activism" (Towner 1987, 99) is small and logical. Paul's teaching had stated the social, racial and sexual barriers were nothing in the community of faith (Gal.3:28, Col. 3:11, 1 Cor. 12:13). As a consequence The Corinthian women were upsetting the balance in the community (1 Cor. 11:2-16 13:33-35). If not already active, it was at least an anticipated probability that it would spread to the slaves (I Cor. 7:17-24). Paul wrote to the church attempting to bring the enthusiasts' equality back into balance. Three times he advises the groups in the church to stay as they are (7:17, 20, 24).

The author of the Pastorals is concerned about social balance as well as the heresy and we see very similar themes addressed in the Pastorals as in 1 Corinthians. Here in Ephesus women and slaves were also causing problems in the church. The women are told to dress appropriately and were not allowed to have authority over men (1 Tim. 2:9-15). Slaves were commanded to respect and obey their masters (1 Tim. 6:1-2; cf. Titus 2:9-10). There may also have been problems in the family (1 Tim. 2:15; 3:4-5, 12; 5:4, 8,16; Titus 2). Can the social problems be related to the heresy?

We can be certain that the false teachers arose out of the community itself as;

- o Timothy and Titus were told (1 Tim. 1:3, Titus 1: 5-11) to instruct these teachers which would suggest that they were identifiable in the Christian community.

- o Paul's prophesy about some falling away from the faith in the last days 1 Tim.4.1 was meant to be relevant to the present situation as well, implying again that the teachers came from amongst them.

- o They are also described as having deviated from the faith 1 Tim 1:6, 6:21, 2 Tim 2:18

- o In Paul's farewell to the Ephesian elders he said that error would arise from among them (Acts 20:30).

We can also have some understanding of their methods. They were finding openings in the household – upsetting whole households in the process (2 Tim. 3:6; Titus 1:11). Many women were targeted and some were succumbing to the heresy (2 Tim.3:6, 1 Tim. 5:15) but it was not only women who accepted the teaching as its ringleaders were men. These men, deceived by demons and with a seared conscience, were equated to the worst sinners of the end times. Their motive was greed (Titus 1:11; 1 Tim. 6:5,9) which they could no longer see as their conscience was seared (1 Tim. 4:1-2). This is totally different language to that used of the women. The view of feminine evil where women are weak[56,] and more impressionable and impulsive than men, and so more likely to sin than men, can not be supported by this and other passages in the Pastorals. While these women probably disseminated the teaching, it was men who led the heresy, Hymenaeus, Philetus and Alexander. These were not the powerful women held in high regard by the New Testament writers and they are not called weak but "little, silly women" (Geitz 1991, 111).

---

[56] Words used to translate the "silly women" of the NRSV are "weak willed" RSV and "weak" NASB

Teaching of emancipation must have been attractive to women in a city with its founding associated with the Amazons and the prominent role given to women in the imperial cult and at the temple of Artemis Ephesia. The desire for emancipation without obedience and responsibility is stifled and Paul calls the women of both Corinth and Ephesus back to "the culturally acceptable role and conduct of women" (Towner 1987, 111) (1 Tim. 2:8-15, 1 Cor. 14:33-35). It is understandable that young widows might not want to marry and saw "Christian widowhood as the best means of independence from marriage and family life" (Padgett 1987, 21). It was a deeper issue though than just independence as they were neglecting to support their own mothers (1 Tim. 5:16).[57] Instead we find a readiness to support the heretical teachers. We find also that modesty in attire, a "Greco-Roman virtue in women" (Padgett 1987, 23) also is wanting. The advice on what not to wear (1 Tim 2:9) shows these women were wealthy and so more likely to have home churches and want leadership roles (Padgett 1987, 23).

To crown all this, the false teachers claimed that they had a special gnosis (1 Tim. 6:2), the only heretical doctrine actually named in the Pastorals. This word causes many to look to Gnosticism in some form as the heresy. This word itself cannot justify that assumption as it was also a word from the Biblical tradition. Gnosticism was a knowledge that "released the soul from enslavement to the material world" (Towner 1987, 104). All of Gnosticism was directed at understanding who man is, in contrast to Biblical knowledge which "focused on God, what he has done, and what he demands" (Towner 1987, 104). Completely missing is

---

[57] This neglect of parents can be seen in The Acts of Paul and Thecla 43.

the speculative cosmology of the aeon and archon.[58]   The salvific power associated with the possession of this gnosis in developed Gnosticism is missing.

The gnosis instead appears to be the belief that the resurrection was already past (2 Tim. 2:18).   This is not a denial of the resurrection of believers but a spiritualising of the event as is implied with the perfect tense of gegonenai, and claiming future benefits now.   This gnosis that the resurrection was past is best regarded as a special insight, not something "'to be experienced through the reception of the gnosis" (Towner 1987, 107).   This is closer to the use of the word in Corinth and Colossae than Gnosticism. This belief could have arisen from a misunderstanding of Paul's preaching that the believer had been raised in Christ (Rom 6:8).

At this stage the idea that all foods were created clean was accepted Christian doctrine having been taught by Jesus (Lk. 11:40-41, Mk. 7:15) and also Paul (1 Cor. 8-10 c.f. Rom. 14). Later Gnostics would refrain from certain foods because of their distaste of the material because of its creation by the evil Demiurge. However the abstinence of certain foods does not make the heretics Gnostic. If the eschatological future could be drawn into the present it would be sufficient explain the promotion of abstinence from foods as they represented the old order (Towner 1987, 108).   This could probably be described as an "eschatological dualism" (Towner 1987, 108) but it does not derive from a belief that matter was evil because of an evil creator.

---

[58] The meanings of these terms varied greatly among the multitude of Gnostic systems. Generally it was believed that spirit was good and matter was evil and the divine being had to be separated from it through a series of intermediaries.

Where did the restrictions on marriage (1 Tim. 4:3 c.f. Titus 4:3) originate? Prohibitions on marriage were a part of some form of gnosticism but this was probably a feature of the Essenes/Qumran covenanters (Towner 1987, 108) and was also present in Corinth. The view in Corinth and Ephesus that the Eschaton had passed would have been enough to explain the prohibition of marriage in both cities. Marriage in the new order would be unspiritual and the teaching of Jesus himself could be used as evidence.

The knowledge that the resurrection had passed, with its implications for an over realised eschatology could produce opposite effects just as Gnosticism could produce opposite effects. In Corinth, which appears to be free of a Judaizing influence, it produced "liberty" while in Ephesus it was restraint.

Paul counters this in 2 Tim. 2:8-13. Paul emphasises the resurrection of Christ, not the believer and the hymn states that the salvation entered into is not complete and that the believer must endure faithfully to the end. The Pastorals show the normal "categories of pre-history, the present age and eschatological Day and age to come" (Towner 1987, 113). Certainly the appearing of Christ has changed the world but not in the sense of the Jewish eschatological hope where all the wrongs of this world would be righted on one great day. The changes wrought by Christ are unfinished and while this is an age of salvation, the nature of this world is still evil and the believer must endure to the end. The trials of this world are only meaningful in light of a second epiphany and like the first that was not done in a corner, (Acts 26:26) This will also be an historical event. Paul does not know of a spiritualised resurrection. This is very different to the heretics view who have everything now and so have "upset the balance between the 'already/not yet' in the community's thinking" (Towner 1987, 114).

A major difference between Corinth and Ephesus is that Corinth did not seem to have an emphasis on the Law (Mounce 2000, lxxiv).

Comparison to the Colossian Heresy

Colossae was another major city in Asia Minor and with Ephesus shared a syncretistic culture (Mounce 2000, lxxiii). It is not surprising that we see some similarities. Paul's response to heresy is very different in the Pastorals to that in Colossians leading some to see this as evidence against Paul's authorship. In the former he denounces heresy, in the latter he refutes it. In Colossians, Paul was writing to a church, which he had probably never visited and gives very careful instruction on the nature of the heresy and shows what course their belief should follow. In the Pastorals Paul writes to his associates, who already had intimate observation of the way the apostle refuted heresy, advising what actions they must take (Guthrie 1957, 38). A major difference in Colossae s that the heresy did seem to be more defined (Mounce, 2000, lxxiii) so there was actually something to attack.

It is thought that the Colossian heresy involved magic (Towner 2000, lxxiii) as it is described as "philosophy and empty deceit, according to the elemental spirits of the universe" (Col .2:8) which was "not according to Christ." "who had disarmed the principalities and powers" (Col. 2:15). This heresy minimised the roll of Christ.

Concluding Comments

It is normal to see that there is one heresy at play in the city. Fee for instance views the Ephesian heresy as having affinities with the troubles at Colosse a few years earlier. He suggests that heresy was "probably a form of Hellenistic Judiasm that has imbibed a good deal from Hellenism" (1985, 144). Hellenistic religion explains the mercenary nature of the heretics. A slightly different conclusion is made by Mounce who says it "was much closer to the errors at Colossae and Corinth, mixed with portions of aberrant Judaism, speculative superstition, and possibly magic" (2000, lxxv). The conclusion of both does not require a timing later than Paul.

Ephesus, the home of magic was characterised by widely divergent religions but each had remarkable "religious encounters" [59]. In Hellenistic religion, temples, games, priesthoods, sacrifices and reverence were more important than "emotional sincerity, assent to doctrines, or divine essence" (Friensen U.D., 166). Already the city was looking to build a temple to the Imperial cult and would soon build a complex for a living Emperor and worship him as a god. Did the Greeks believe the emperor was a god? There is no evidence of fulfilled prayer by any emperor, dead or alive (Arnold 1989, 37) but there are records of intense religious experience

---

[59] Refer to my *Ephesus – History and Religious Setting* where these are outlined.

associated with these gods.[60]

We know that many of the early members had imbibed deeply of the religious atmosphere of the town as many had practiced magic and magic scrolls worth 50,000 days wages were burnt by members (Acts 19:19). These were people who had not lived blameless lives as they openly confessed their evil deeds (Acts 19:18 NIV) and turned the faith into an experience. They would also be familiar with the intense religious experiences to offer in the mysteries of the pagan religions surrounding them. It would only be a short jump to attempt to Hellenise Christianity into a religion where Christian terminology was present but only having a shell without its vital core of exclusive and ethical truth.

But was there one heresy or two? Payne claims there was a Judaising group and a libertarian group in the city in which women took prominence (2:9-15, 4:7, 5:6-7) (Payne 1981, 183 & 186). To counter the libertarian group Paul demands that the leaders be above reproach (3:1-13) and all others are called to the same level of godly purity and holiness (2:9, 12, 15; 4:7, 8, 12; 5:7). Now good works are to replace idleness (2:10; 5:6-15) (Payne 1981, 186).

---

[60] Harland cites "a letter from an association of Demetriasts in Ephesus to the proconsul of the province of Asia about 88-89 CE . . .. In the letter the Demetriasts make their request as follows: Mysteries and sacrifices are performed each year in Ephesus, lord, to Demeter Karpophoros and Thesmophoros and to the Sebastoi gods by mystai with great purity and lawful customs together with the priestesses" (Harland 1996, 331). Unfortunately we do not know what these mysteries were. Mysteries were also an important part of the worship of Artemis.

Opposing this libertarian trend were Judaisers who were who were consumed by genealogies and controversies (1:4). By imposing the Law excessively (1:9) they asserted male supremacy (2:13-14) and attempted to keep the women from teaching (2:11). Paul does not criticise their respect for the Old Testament scriptures (1:8; 2:13-15; 4:5; 5:18) or angels (3:16; 5:21) but urges then to return to "the pillar and bulwark of the truth" (3:15) of a gospel where God desires everyone to be saved including the gentiles (2:4-7) (Payne 1981, 186). Payne argues that Paul called for concessions from both the parties e.g. to the Jews who traditionally did not let women learn he says to let them learn but as a concession will not allow the immodestly dressed women to teach[61] (Payne 1981, 183).

Alternatively there may have been one heresy, that the resurrection had passed, but that it had two outworkings. One with a libertarian outlook and the other Jewish.

---

[61] Payne tables the advice he maintains is given to each party and to both (1981, 188)

5 IMPERIAL CULT

An inscription found in Priene[62], a city of the Ionian league along with Ephesus says in part "Since Providence, which has ordered all things and is deeply interested in our life, has set in most perfect order by giving us Augustus, whom she filled with virtue that he might benefit humankind, sending him as a savior, [sōtēr], both for us and for our descendants, that he might end war and arrange all things, and since he, Caesar, by his appearance [ejpifanei'n] (excelled even our anticipations), surpassing all previous benefactors, and not even leaving to posterity any hope of surpassing what he has done, and since the birthday of the god Augustus was the beginning of the good tidings for the world that came by reason of him," . . . which Asia resolved in Smyrna" (Boring 1995, 169).

In this inscription we have good news, mediated from the gods through a saviour who has made an appearance on the earth as a powerful ruler who brings peace on earth. So great were his works that they could never be equalled. It is not surprising that with such an understanding of salvation in the pagan world that Paul appears to deliberately confront the imperial cult and the role of emperor as saviour.

Inscriptions have been found in Ephesus, the traditionally accepted destination of 1 and 2 Timothy, of three words saviour, appearance and piety which show a link to the Imperial Cult setting (Gill 2008,

---

[62] Known as the Priene Inscription (*OGIS* 458) and dates at A.D. 9 (Gill 2008, 96).

101).

Saviour, is used twelve times in Paul's epistles, ten of these are in the Pastorals where the word is used of God (1 Tim. 2:3; Titus 2:13) and of Jesus (2 Tim. 1:10; Titus 3:6). The word means "one who rescues, savior, deliverer, preserver" (BDAG 985) and when used of the emperor was commonly linked with "benefactor". For the Graeco-Romans, the "term 'savior' was applied to philosophers, such as Epicurus (P.Hercul. 346.4.19, gods, such as Asclepius (Aelius Aristides. *Orat.* 42.4) and Zeus (*SIG* 985, 60-62) and deified rulers such as Augustine (*OGIS* 458) and Nero (*OGIS* 668)" (Gill 2008, 94). In Ephesus, the term was also frequently used of Artemis but also of the emperors (Gill 2008, 95). An inscription dating to 48 B.C. has been found that refers to Julius Caesar as "the common saviour of mankind". The use of saviour as a designation of a deified ruler though well known earlier is said to have risen to prominence from A.D. 50 onwards (Towner 1989, 76). This idea, if not the actual early inscription referring to Caesar may be reflected in 1 Tim. 4:10 where God is called the saviour of all people. Paul and Timothy would have been very aware of this words prominence in Ephesus.

In the Jewish context this word was used almost exclusively of Yahweh. He had shown what it was to be a saviour when he delivered his people from Egypt. Understandably the term was popular with the Jews but Paul's use seems to be in a way that was culturally significant to his readers (Gill 2008, 94, 97). He simply uses it without any explanation (Trebilco 2004, 361). Towner suggests that the "sudden popularity of the term in certain Christian circles, in a time and location(s) coincident with the influence of the Ruler-Cult, represents an apologetic, polemic, or evangelistic reaction against the competing claims and pressures levelled upon the Christian communities by the Imperial religion" (Towner 1989, 77) As such God, who is the gracious provider of the whole world, is contrasted to the limited benefaction of a deified ruler (Baugh 1992:331-40).

The author of the Pastorals uses appearance ???? 1 Tim. 6:14; 2 Tim. 1:10, 4:1,8 and Titus 2:13 and in Titus 2:11 3:4 the verbal form is found and in each case they refer to Jesus. There are references to both the first appearance of Jesus (2 Tim 1:2; Titus 2:11) and his second (1 Tim. 6:14; 2 Tim. 4:1,8) referred to elsewhere as his parousia. Despite the extensive use of appearance in the Pastorals it is not a major theme in Jewish literature (Marshall 1999, 293-95). Gill concludes that along with sōtēr (savior), a strong case can be made for the Hellenistic background to ejpifanei'n (appearance) where its usual meaning is the "self manifestation of the divine being in the world" (Trebilco 2004, 355). The word is found 59 times in the LXX and 47 of these are in the Hellenistic book of 4 Maccabees (Dibelius and Conzelmann 1972, 37). Some of the emperors would claim this honour while alive; others were deified after their death[63]. In 1 Tim 6:14b-15 the Lord Jesus Christ is the King of Kings and the imperial cult terminology of "appearing" is used of him

The Author of the Pastorals calls the readers "to obedience in light of the impending appearance, not of the emperor but, of the true sovereign Jesus Christ" (Gill 2008, 99). By using the same Hellenistic pattern of thought (Dibelius and Conzelmann 1972,

---

[63] Julius Caesar, Augustus and Claudius were deified after death. The Senate denied this honour to Tiberius, Caligula and Nero. Nero revoked the deity of Claudius

104) and language it suggests that the Hellenistic religion was of concern to the writer and audience (Gill 2008, 99).If so, it would then follow that there is a deliberate contrast between Christianity and the imperial cult.

The noun *eusebeia* is not found in the acknowledged Pauline letters but, with its cognates is common (13 occurrences) in the Pastorals. With a meaning of "piety, reverence, loyalty (exhibited towards parents or deities), fear of God" (BDAG 412) was both a Jewish and Graeco-Roman concept. For the latter it became to mean the actual outward act of worship to the gods (Trebilco 2004, 361) as opposed to the Jewish inner ethical attitude of reverence in Judaism (Marshall 1999, 136-39). By using *eusebeia* the author again may have been tapping into the Hellenistic mindset and redefining the word to have "a distinctly Christian meaning" (Gill 2008, 101). This desirable virtue to which many attained was virtually unachievable (Gill 2008, 151). When calling the believers to *eusebia*, the writer was saying that "higher goals of secular ethics are releasable only in Christ" (Marshall 1999, 424). Christians were to live as model citizens, praying for their emperor, so showing what true piety was through their godly "living under the true Saviour of humanity" (Gill 2008, 152).

The term "mediator" (μεσίτης) is generally believed to have derived from μέσος meaning "middle" or "among" and was used with the meanings of "judging between us" and "umpire". The noun mediator is "relatively widely" used in the ancient world in a wide range of religious and non-religious settings (Gill 2008, 112). Its principal meaning is peacemaker with later meanings of "guarantor" or "witness" or to the introduction of two parties, one of whom is usually a deity (Gill 2008, 113). Because references to

Jesus as mediator are uncommon in the New Testament (1 Tim. 2:5, Gal. 3:19-20, Heb. 8:6, 9:15, 12:24) and rare in the Apostolic Fathers, Gill then questions whether the word was deliberately avoided.

Because the Graeco-Roman world had numerous deities and diverse religious practices, there was a widespread and contradictory views about how this mediation took place (Gill 2008, 114). In Judaism a paid priest, whose eligibility to perform the task was laid out in the Law was needed to present an offering to God. Kings and prophets might reveal god's will "ultimately the individuals had to come to God through the mediating work of priests" (Gill 2008, 123). While the idea of mediation is common in the OT, the word for mediator is only found once in the LXX in Job 9:33. The word "angel" often carried the connotation of a mediator and Moses was extraordinary in the way he fulfilled this role (Philo *De Vita Mosis*, 2:166). In the Graeco-Roman world there was little agreement on who could be a priest and normally they were not paid (Gill 2008, 115). They did not normally fulfil the role of mediator as an offering could be made direct to his/her deity (Gill 2008, 115). In the classical period the senate was "the major group to claim the role if mediator between humanity and the gods" (Gill 2008, 116). They would not understand the separation of church and state as their decisions mediated the decisions of god (Gill 2008, 116).

The end of the republic saw a rise of people who tried to seek god without the mediation of the governing powers but the rise of the emperor saw a trend to re-establish the old form of mediation. The belief arose that the emperor alone was the *Pontifex Maximus*[64] (chief priest) between humanity and the gods (Gill 2008, 116-7). This role was promoted through inscriptions in public places and temples and the widespread distribution of coins. This constant declaration of the emperor's role as chief priest gradually gained acceptance leading to the growth of the provincial cults and the priesthood to service them (Gill 2008, 119-20). Through his power to tax the various temples the emperor virtually controlled the cults and showed their subordination to him (Gill 2008, 121).

At the time the Pastorals were written, the imperial religious indoctrination was being accepted in Ephesus and by the end of the century it was as prominent as the worship of Artemis. Her worship had even taken elements of the imperial cult (Gill 2008, 104). The cult was being driven home by a public rebuilding of large parts of the city in ways that honoured the Emperor. By the time Ephesus had her official provincial cult there were already 50 statues of the emperor (Strelan 1996, 110-12), one as high as 7 metres high (Gill 2008, 105). His image or name would possibly be seen at each turn (Gill 2008, 105). The traditional dating of Revelation would place it just after the approval for imperial cult and some would see numerous references to it in the Revelation, particularly 2:1-7.

Augustus was seen as a saviour who had made war to cease To pray "to" or "on behalf of" the emperor was to seek blessing from the gods through the mediation of blessing provided by the Roman emperor and his empire" (Gill 2008, 143).

---

[64] Augustus revived this title in 12 B.C. He was after all the son of a god so there must have been a divine element to his reign (Gill 2008, 118).

The reference to Jesus that sees him as mediator (1 Tim. 2:5) should be seen as taking a known practice in the writer's society and correcting it (Gill 2008, 143)

6. OPINION OF UNBELIEVERS

Throughout the three Pastoral Epistles, each group is called to exemplary behaviour. Paul is very concerned about the opinion that society in general had of the believers. Elders had to be "well thought of by outsiders" and disgrace was to be avoided as it was not just loosing face but the snare of the devil (1 Tim. 3:7). The older women were to train the young women in their responsibilities as wives and mothers "so that the word of God may not be discredited" (Titus 2:5). Similarly young widows were to "give the enemy no opportunity for slander" (I Tim. 5:14). How Christian this behaviour is has been questioned. Koester writes, "Christianity no longer looked upon itself as a religious sect with a divine calling that required commitment to unusual ethical demands. Rather, the church had become obligated to the world and society at large and had to fulfil the general social norms in an exemplary fashion (1982, 302).

The lives of young men were to be a "model of good works" and their faith seen through "sound speech that cannot be censured; then any opponent will be put to shame, having nothing evil to say of us." (Titus 2:8). Despite their lowly social status, Christian slaves were not exempt and they also must be held in high regard so "the name of God and the teaching may not be blasphemed" (1 Tim. 6:1). This respect could not be earned if they did not hold their masters in high regard. Their good service and honesty would show this respect and "that in everything they may be an ornament to the doctrine of God our Saviour" (Titus 2:10).

Because when "the grace of God has appeared, bringing salvation to all" (Titus 2:11), Paul taught that there was an equality that cut across every social division that existed in the city. This radical equality was open to great abuse (Tim. 6:2) and would work against the church if there was not an equality "in the high standard of Christian character and intercourse in the church as the family of God" (Lock 1978, 3). Permeating this call to develop Christian character is the expectation that the church would be a teaching community in which all are involved. Elders are teaching the church, old women were to teach teaching what is good not just in their family but to the young wives. Young men were to teach with integrity and gravity (Titus 2:6). Only slaves are not mentioned as having a teaching role.

7. ESCHATOLOGY OF THE PASTORALS

In the Gospels there is a tension between the immanent and delayed return of Christ. When Luke wrote his gospel there was a belief that the return was near but this is not present in Acts. Presumably some time had elapsed between his writing of the Gospel and Acts which may account for this change of emphasis. The Lord is certainly returning (Acts 1:6-8) but time is now allowed to evangelize the Gentiles. Paul's long connection with Luke may be influential in this change of view.

It has been argued that in the Pastorals the tension is no longer present as the belief in the imminent return has disappeared making the Pastorals very much like Acts in their eschatology (Wilson 1979, 12). While others argue to the contrary it seems hard to deny that the overall picture of the Pastorals is that the church is "settling in" and developing institutions that will prepare it for long term stability. In Hebrews there is an obvious disappointment among believers that the parousia has not occurred.

This disappointment is not seen in Luke or the Pastorals and probably reflects the importance placed on the Gentile ministry by these men. Both Luke and the Pastorals use the living and the dead to describe those who will be judged by Christ (Acts 10:42; 2 Tim. 4:1) and both also use the words *epiphainein, epiphaneia* and *epiphanes*[65]. It is used elsewhere only in 2 Thess. 2:8. In the Pastorals the term can refer to the parousia (1 Tim. 6:14; 2 Tim.

---

65 This similarity leads Wilson to suggest that there might be a common authorship (1972, 19)

4:1; Titus 2:13) and the incarnation (2 Tim. 1:10, 4:8; Titus 2:11, 3:4). Luke uses the word differently though, in the gospel it refers to salvation bought by Jesus (Luke 1:79) and in Acts it is a reference to judgment day (Acts 2:20).

The Spirit had expressly said that that in the last days men would follow false teachers (1 Tim. 4:1ff). This is possibly a reference to Christian prophesy as the rise of false teachers before the end is a Christian e.g. Mark 13.22 rather than Jewish characteristic (Wilson 1972, 14). The rise of false teachers does not however necessarily mean that the end times were at hand. The phrase en *husterois kairois* while sometimes translated as last days[66] is probably better translated as "later" (NRSV and NIV) or "future times" and so is looking to the ongoing life of the church. While they are spoken of as a future threat in 1 Timothy 4 it has become a real danger in 2 Timothy 3 1-6.

Paul believed he was living in the last days (note the shift from the future tense in 2 Timothy 3 1-5 to the present tense in verse 6) but how imminent was this end? The Pastorals appear to be dealing with a church which Paul envisions as being around for a long time. Wilson notes "the main emphasis of the Pastorals is practical, concentrating on the organization and smooth functioning of the Church and the establishment of good relations with the world." (1972 15).

What is understood by in the last days? The same phrase occurs in Acts 2:17-20 and here we see an extended period of ministry of the

---

66 This would make 1 Tim 4:1 a synonym for 2 Tim 3:6

spirit that permeates the whole earth not just a few elect. There is a hint that this may occur in Stephen's lifetime "I charge you[14] to keep the commandment without spot or blame until the manifestation of our Lord Jesus Christ" (2 Tim 6:14). The verse goes on to emphasise that this will happen at the proper time. While they may well have been surprised at how long the parousia has taken there is no disappointment about the time scale and there is no doubt it is something which will certainly come to pass (Titus 2:13). There only the need to counteract and contradict the false teaching that the resurrection had passed (2 Tim 2:18).

The eschatological hope represented in Acts and the Pastorals is represented by the following illustration67:

The Eschaton

begun   consumated

THIS AGE   (passing away)

THE AGE TO COME   (never ending)

the Cross   the Second
and   Comming
Ressurection

---

67 Fee. *Corinthians...*, 85.

8. CHURCH OFFICERS

From the start of his missions trips Paul was concerned about good governance in the churches. Most likely with the established and proven pattern of governance in the synagogue as a pattern Paul appointed elders at the earliest possibility (Acts 14:23) and elders were known to have been established early in the church in Ephesus (Acts 20:17). Surprisingly, in the acknowledged Pauline epistles there is very little reference to the officers of the church.[68] In the Ephesian epistle it refers to pastors and teachers which approximate the roles we encounter in the Pastorals. Depending on how we assess the historicity of the Pastorals will determine whether the ecclesiastical setting we see in them is just an anachronism or an apostolic model. In opposition to this, some would see the early church as a charismatic and Spirit infused organism that avoided formal structure for over fifty years (Mounce 2000, lxxxvi-lxxxvii).

Is there a problem with a sophisticated system of church government occurring during Paul's lifetime? Organisation would have been essential as the church progressed from having a developing tradition guided by apostolic witness to local leaders who were tradition bearers: e.g., 2 Tim.2:2; Tit. 1:9 (Guthrie 1957, 29). This is more than organising the church; it is about reforming it (Fee 1985, 147). The Churches with an emphasis on charisma had proven to be fraught with problems[69]. An ill-disciplined charismatic membership in Corinth had caused major problems

---

68 Leading to the suggestion that the Acts references are anachronistic (Guthrie, 1990, 625).

69 Views that see the church organisation in the Pastorals generally invoke special pleading by expunging from Acts the references to Paul and Barbabus appointing elders (Guthrie 1957, 27)

and now ill-disciplined elders were leading the church astray in Ephesus. Yet even in this church there were believers with the spiritual gift of administration (1 Cor. 12:28). Secular organisational skills were sophisticated enough to run an empire stretching from Britain to Egypt. In Ephesus the Apostle was friends with the Asiarchs (Acts 19:31) who organised large games at a time when Ephesus was "crowded to capacity with hordes of people from all over Ionia" (Barclay 1973, 119). What calibre of people did the Ephesian church contain? They had certainly more than enough skill to organise a church specially when they had the model of the synagogue to follow and now knew what problems they had to confront.

Church government is different in 1 Timothy to Titus. Paul had spent an extended period in Ephesus, sufficient time to develop a structure with overseers and deacons. Yet despite Paul's regular teaching, many of them simply had not learned the gospel (Mounce 2000, lvii). Poor leadership has allowed the false teachers to develop such a strong foothold. Establishing a functioning church government is critical in Ephesus and twenty seven of the 113 verses of 1 Timothy deal with it (Mounce 2000, lix). In Crete, which appears to be a much younger church, only elders are appointed without deacons (Tit 1:5). This suggests that deacons are only appointed after the church grows. Church government was much less an issue as it is only the subject of five verses out of forty-six.

It has been observed that for the officers in the church:

- o The qualifications are primarily moral as the behaviour of the officer should validate the message he brings;

- o The officers are seen sometimes as servants and other times as members of God's household, and o The actual requirements of and interplay between different members in a household (e.g. slave, mother, father, elderly, young) apply metaphorically to the church officers (Pietersen 1994, 98-99).

Virtue and vice lists were characteristic of Hellenistic paraenesis. Paul made a habit of making virtue and vice lists in which Christian content was put in Hellenistic paraenetic form (Gordon 2002, 109-10) .The formalised lists of virtues and vices we see in the Pastorals are not like anything in the Old Testament. There are short lists of vices (Prov. 6:17-19, Jer. 7:9, Hos. 4:2) but perhaps there is little need to list the virtues as the Covenant, either in its concentrated form and in the myriad of laws required a universal high standard for priest and laity alike. Because of this difference, some see these lists as representing Hellenistic, rather than Biblical values. They are no more than a "floating list of vices currently available and easily adaptable to the writer's purpose, a whiplash of stringing words of the sort that any orator of the time well understood where to get and how to use" (Gealy 1955, 498). This view would make these lists no more than an attempt to gain respectability and peace in a pagan world (Dibelius and Conzelmann 1972, 8-10, 39, 141)

It may well be possible that Paul was aware of the numerous parallels in pagan (Diogenes Laertius VII 116ff; Onasander Stratego 1:2-17), Christian (Polycarp, Epistle to the Philippians) and Jewish (Community Rule 4 of the Essenes Community Rule) sources. A close similarity is claimed[70] with the description of a

---

[70] Two of the eleven words in Onsander's list are the same as Paul's list and three are similar, but there are also differences such as an ability to teach, not an excessive wine drinker, and his ability to govern his family as evidence of his ability to govern the church. Whereas the military general should neither be too young or too old, Paul is interested in Christian maturity (Mappes 2003, 212).

general in Onsander's Stratego where he starts saying "I believe, then that we must choose a general, not because of noble birth as priests are chosen, nor because of wealth as superintendents of the gymnasia, but because he is temperate, self-restrained, vigilant, frugal, hardened to labour, alert, free from avarice, neither too young nor too old, indeed a father of children if possible, a ready speaker, and a man with a good reputation."[42] and then elaborates on each of these virtues.

The comparison between the ideal general and the ideal elder in not accidental. The church is seen at war, (1 Tim. 1:18, Eph. 9:7, 2 Tim. 2:3) and the elders are its generals, with God the Commander in Chief. The use of Bishop, always in the singular may permit that the office be understood in the light of a presiding elder.

In the qualifications for office bearers there is no mention of the possession of the Spirit (c.f. Acts 6:3) or of the intellectual capacity of the office bearers. These two characteristics, desirable as they are, are very hard to measure objectively and may well have been deliberately omitted by Paul. The clear evidence of the possession of the Spirit as seen in the original deacons was now muddied. The "possession" of the Spirit in Corinth was no longer a reliable sign of true spirituality. Cleverness alone was no sign of fitness for office as a false Intellectualism was taking the Ephesian church into heresy.

The dissimilarities are so striking that it is hard to argue dependence.
[42] Oldfather, suggests that Stratego was written in about A.D. 58 (1923, 347 n. 3).

Paul is establishing a framework based on the imitation but, are the requirements for office simply striving for middle class respectability based on imitating an Hellenistic standard (Mounce 2003, 208)? The model clearly does have similarities with the Hellenistic virtues but there is nothing in the Pastorals that show the ethic of the church has changed. This ethic was one of difference and change leading to severance from paganism on one hand and from gross Christian error on the other. This framework was one whereby true spirituality and possession of true knowledge can be judged. This was found not in copying the best of the Hellenistic world but through the imitation of the example of trusted officers. In a sense the guidelines are qualifications, not to be a ruler but to be a role model. A smaller church than that at Ephesis may have little need of administrators but the role model remains crucially important.

Paul had called on the church to imitate him (Phil. 3:17) and also his companions, Timothy and Sylvanus (1 Thess. 1:6-7) as in so doing they would be imitating Christ. By this imitation of the ethical uprightness Paul-who-was-imitating-Christ (1 Cor. 11:1) would "provide a sense of unity" to the young church (Mappes 2003, 217). This imitation would not be of the apostles' personality and gifts and mannerisms but of more weighty matters. These include

- o Joyful endurance of suffering (1 Thess. 1:6)

- o Industry and self sacrifice (2 Thess. 3:7)

- o Humility and self giving (1 Cor. 4;15-16)

- o Relinquishing of rights (1 Cor. 9:1-11.1)

- o Complete commitment to Christ (Phil. 3:12-17)

But with Paul's imminent death and the foreseeable departure and eventual death of his companions this model would soon be passing. Church officers had progressed from imitating the Apostles to being an example themselves. This imitation is not a two tiered arrangement with a lesser standard for members. Imitation is at the core of the Lord's Prayer and is far more radical than anything Paul said. In the prayer there is no imitation of Christ, or an apostle but the Father is asked to imitate the believer. Gregory of Nyssa wrote "Jesus wants your disposition to be a good example to God. We invite God to imitate us. Do thou the same as I have done. Imitate thy servant O Lord. Though he be only a poor beggar and though art the King of the universe. I have shown great mercy to my neighbour imitate thy servants charity" (quoted Barclay 1964,) .This is the standard of imitation called for every believer.

The Role of Timothy and Titus

The words used in the Pastoral Epistles to describe the officers of the church, bishop and presbyters/elders and deacons have become familiar to us through Catholicism. It is far from certain that the terms of the modern Episcopal system mean the same as they did in the first century. Frequently the terms bishop and presbyter as used in the Pastorals are seen not as separate offices but rather the one group with the bishop being "the president of the college of elders" (Pietersen 1994, 98). Ignatius (died between A.D. 98 – A.D. 117) in his letter argues so strongly for the episcope[71] that it suggests that the role was not universally accepted.

---

[71] See Letter to the Smyrnaeans 8

Under the Ignatian style episcopal system Timothy and Titus would be seen as acting as a Metroploitan, Timothy over the Ephesian community and Titus over Crete. Evidence for this is seen in that:

o They received their authority at ordination

o They are of higher rank than the elders

o They appoint and discipline elders

o They are responsible instruction and discipline (Guthrie, 1957, 30)

While all this is agreed there is no evidence to see them as anything other than apostolic delegates, representing the apostle to the Gentiles (Guthrie 1990, 627). They are fulfilling a role similar to the ones already exercised in Macedonia and Achia (Guthrie 1990, 627). Arguing against the monarchical episcopate is failure to mention that only one elder (bishop) is to be appointed in each church as the term bishop is used indiscriminately with elders. The responsibility of a church (or home church) did not rest with an individual but a group. Apart from Philippians 1:1 there is no other supporting reference to the titles overseers and deacons, and this verse gives no indication of their actual duties. It does however show that plural leadership was not unique to Ephesus and Crete. Paul also gives no instruction about how to perpetuate this role.

Paul had shown what it was to minister with a clear conscience and behaviour that was above reproach. Timothy and Titus were not put forward to show us what a pastor is like (Fee 1985, 147). In Paul's absence both Timothy and Titus were to again provide proper examples of what Christ was like (2 Tim 1:14; Titus 2:7-8).

This role was very important when there were now competing voices as to who represented Christ.

The qualifications for church office from the Pastorals is listed below

The Qualifications of Church Officers and their Nature				
Episkopoi in 1 Timothy 3	Diakonoi in 1 Timothy 3	Presbyteroi in Titus	All Women72	Nature
They desire a "good work" 3:1 kalou ergou			2:10 ergōn agathōn 5:10 ergois kalois	
1. General Requirements ... All Positive				
(1) Christian Morality in General				
(a) Above reproach, unassailable v2 anepilēmpton	Worthy of respect v8	Must be blameless v6	5:7 anepilēmptoi	Moral
(b) Married once v2 mias gynaikos andra	Married once	Husband of one wife v6	5:9 henos andros gynē	Moral

---

72 Payne, *Liberterian...*, 194.

			3:11 nēphalious	Moral
(c) Temperate v2 nēphalion			3:11 nēphalious	Moral
(d) Self Control v2 sōphrona		Not quick tempered v7 self controlled v8	2:9, 15 sōphrosynēs	Moral
(e) Respectable and virtuous v2 kosmion	Sincere v8	loves what is good v8	2:9 kosmein	Moral
(2) Morality in Relation to the Church				
(a) Hospitable v2 philoxenon		Hospitable v8	5:10 eteknotrophēsen, thlibomenois epērkesen	Spiritual
(b) Able to teach v2 didaktikon	Hold the deep truths with a clear conscience v9	Hold deep truths so he can encourage and refute v9	2:11 manthanetō cf. 1:7 (τις)́ nomodidaskaloi cf. Titus 2:3 kalodidaskalous 3:3 mē paroinon	Spiritual

2. Detailed Requirements - Mainly Negative				
(1) In daily life				
(a) Little wine v3 mē plēktēn	Little wine v8	Not given to drunkenness v7	3:11 nēphalious cf. Titus 2:3 mē oinō pollō dedoulōmenas	Moral
(b) Not violent but gentle v3 mē plēktēn alla epieikē		Not overbearing v7	2:15 agapē … hagiasmō sōphrosynēs 3:11 mē diabolous cf. Titus 3:2 (for all people) amachous	Moral
(c) Not quarrelsome v3 amachon		Not violent v7	3:11 mē diabolous cf. Titus 3:2 (for all) amachous	Moral
(2) In Relation to the Church				
(a) Not a lover of money v3 aphilargyron	No dishonest gain v8	Not pursuing dishonest gain v7	2:9 mē … chrysiō ē margaritais ē polytelei 3:11 pistas en pasin 6:6–10 (for all) [mē] philargyria	Moral
(b) manages his family v4 tou idiou oikou kalōs	Manages his household v12	Children who believe v6	5:14 oikodespotein cf. Eph 6:1–2	Moral

proistamenon tekna echonta en hypotagē meta pasēs semnotētos			5:14 teknogonein oikodespotein 3:11 semnas	
(c) Not a recent convert v6 mē neophyton	must first be tested v10	Holy v8	5:11 [mē] neōteras cf. 2:15; 5:5, 9	Spiritual
(d) Not proud v6 mē typhōtheis			2:9 en katastolē kosmiō meta aidous … mē himatismō polytelei 2:11 en pasē hypotagē 5:10 podas enipsen	
(e Good reputation v7 enipsen kalēn echein apo tōn exōthen		Upright v8	3:11 semnas	Moral
(4) The Consequences of Failure				
(a receive same penalty as Devil v6 eis krima empesē tou			5:12 krima 5:15 exetrapēsan opisō tou satana	

diabolou				
(b Fall into disgrace v7 mē eis oneidismon empesē			5:14–15 [mē] didonai tō antikeimenō loidorias	
(c Fall into the Devil's trap v7 kai pagida tou diabolou			5:14–15 charin … exetrapēsan opisō tou satana	

Table 4. Qualifications of church office.

The Episkopos

The descriptions of all the officers are so general that it is difficult to draw specific conclusions about their roles or even sex. Apart from Christ, there are never any names associated with this office so there is not any clear evidence that an overseer cannot be a woman[73] (Payne 1981, 195). The other Pauline books give no further information their roles. Unfortunately for Ignatius his views on succession[74] can gain little support from the Pastorals as

---

[73] "The Greek, however has not even one masculine pronoun or possessive, nor any other grammatical specification that Paul had men and not women in mind" (Payne 1981, 196).

[74] Fee observes correctly that church history has shown that succession has had more to do with persons and structures rather than truth. He believes that the New Testament functions as the apostolic succession (1985, 150). He goes on to say, again correctly, that while succession may be denied in theory it is practiced in "little dictatorships" and a ""pluralism of papacies especially in

they deal with primarily with who the *episkopos* is, rather than what he did. The qualifications describe a generally virtuous person who could just as easily be a pagan as a Christian. Onosander's example of a good general has already been given, at the other end of pagan professional life Lucians's description of a good dancer reflects some of the same high moral standards (Dibelius and Conzelmann 1972, 160)[75] The word, frequently translated overseer, means simply that and describes a person who is attentive to things or persons (Mappes 1997, 164). From its use in the Septuagint[76] and Josephus[77] the "term implies general or specific oversight by political, religious, communal, military or municipal individuals (Mappes 1997, 164-5).

What we see of him (the word is always in the singular) is that "in some sense he was the public face of the church" (Pietersen 1994, 100) It could be argued that the singular reference is not so much to one person but to the model overseer. As such he was to be *anepilēmptos* 1 Tim. 3:2ff meaning "one who has nothing which an adversary could seize upon with which to base a charge." (Zodhiates 2000, ref 423). Titus 1:7ff uses the synonym *anenkletos*. Such a man can bear public examination. Their self control in all their life including alcohol would have been recognized by their society as classical Greek virtues (Pietersen 1994, 100) and as such he would be seen as *kosmi*os or respectable. The pastoral moral requirements are strongly reflected in

---

independent churches (1985, 150). This could be avoided if the pastoral pattern of plural leadership serving under accountability and servanthood is followed (Fee 1985, 150-1).

[75] Texts of pagan moral values can be found in Dibelius and Conzelmannn's The Pastoral Epistles P 158-60.

[76] The word covers priestly oversight (Num. 4:16), military leadership (Num. 31:14), stewards (Jud. 9:28) and also the superintendants of those who repaired the Temple (2 Chr. 34:12,17).

[77] The Antiquities of the Jews 10:53; 12:254; 16:321

Polycarp's Letter to Philippians (11:2). The *episkopos* is reasonable in all his dealings, impossible if he was quarrelsome.

The emphasis on the need for exemplarity behaviour contrasts that of the false teachers (1 Tim. 3:1-7, Titus 1:5-9). Likewise the call to moderation in the leaders stands against the aesthetic behaviour of the heretics (1 Tim. 4:3).

The qualifications are linked back to the domestic setting. The *episkopos* is to be hospitable, a virtue commonly extolled (and open to abuse) in early church literature (Didache 11-13 1 Clement 1, 10, 11, 12). Hospitality would have been very important "given the mobility and networking of those early communities, with their travelling apostles, prophets etc" (Pietersen 1994, 100). The ideal domestic scene is continued with the *episkopos* being the husband of one wife and governing his family well who in turn respect him. As with self control this was recognized by the Greeks as a virtue (Isocretes Ad Nioclem 19). As the head of the family as considerable power so the *episkopos* is also seen as having real authority over God's household (Pietersen 1994, 101).

Fulfilling the roll of *episcopos* is a good work, which could also be the same term used of the actions of the benefactors of Ephesus whose public generosity stood testimony to them. All are encouraged to aspire to this position 1 Tim 3:1. The teaching role is important but not stressed in 1 Timothy. There is a warning not to aspire to the role of teacher (Jas 3;1) as the ability to teach without the life that is without reproach is seen as bringing danger of God's judgment. Here there is no warning against aspiring to the role of *episkopos*. The development of the exceptional life should take priority of the development of teaching skills as the life will be what protects the teacher in his teaching and allow the *episcopos* to stand before God without reproof at the judgment. Such character development is impossible in a new convert. The role of the *episcopos* as a teacher is more important in Titus 1:6ff but the crisis caused by those who were spreading false teachings also seems more pressing 1:10-13. There it is the natural outworking of holding the deep truths he has been taught 1:9.

The function of the *episcopos* is most clearly seen in his role as *theou oikonomos*, steward of God, Titus 1:7. Slaves who had the role of business manager of the household were commonly known as *oikonomos*[78]. While the language is that of slavery, they exercised considerable power as their owner's authority and power was entrusted to them. This power is not that of a son who has it by right but of delegated power and because it is delegated the *episcopos* must be chosen who will "set the moral tone of the community" (Pietersen 1994, 103). Again also the imagery of the household is used and the *episcopos* is the one who keeps an eye on God's family.

The role of the *episcopos* as standing in for God as a bishop is developed by Ignatius (Magenesians 6, Trallians 3) but it is far from certain that the *episcopos* has this exulted role in the Pastorals. He has been described far less glamorously as the chief cook and bottle washer (Pietersen 1994, 104). Acts 20 clearly shows that this is not a single person (Fee 1985, 142)

The Presbyteroi

---

[78] This is based on the inscriptions on the tombs of slaves who have recorded their occupation (Pietersen 1994, 102)

The understanding of the role of the different church officers would be much simpler if it was not for Titus. In 1 Tim. 3 there is no *presbyteroi,* referring there only to the *episkopos* and the *diakonoi.* The word does appear in 5:1 where the context is clearly simply an old man who is worthy of respect. This is similar to the way the word is used in Titus 2 where the elderly just like the *episkopos* should be setting a good example. *Diakoni* appears again in 5:17 where the good *presbyteroi* are worth double pay or honour for their ruling, preaching and teaching. This then is a definite role beyond simply being old men.

The term *presbyteroi* is used in the gospels for the elders of the Jewish people which was a position that existed from before the exodus. in the Septuagint זָקֵן is translated by πρεσβύτης or πρεσβύτερος. Josephus also uses this word to describe the Sanhedrin. This council was normally called in Greek the *gerousia* which implies that the members were elderly, experienced and wise senior citizens (Pietersen 1994, 109).

Their greater age[79] means that these men had more than just training, they had maturity and experience. This is mirrored in the life of Jesus who had great knowledge at the age of twelve but still had to grow in wisdom and stature before he could commence his ministry.

---

[79] The elders were actually older but not necessarily "ancient". Glasscock points to a number of Jewish sources that allow leadership positions to be held at 30 and with Christ's ministry also starting at 30 it is probably the minimum age envisaged. Surprisingly Paul and Timothy at this age are still called young men!

Their ruling and teaching role would allow for the words *episkopos* and *presbyteroi* to be simple synonyms and the episkopos (always in the singular) to be the leader of the *presbyteroi*. In 1 Tim 5:19 Paul deals with charges against them, and they can only be accused by two or more witnesses. This special treatment is frequently understood as the discipline of the clergy (Pietersen 1994, 106). A suggestion put forward to explain the role of the presbyteroi is to see them as older members of the community that were especially good as being bearers of the corporate memory and teachers of the tradition for which they received some financial reward (Pietersen 1994, 107). This then would suggest that their office is not at the same level as the *episkopos* but other verses work against this. Their role included presiding (1 Tim. 5:17) and it was this group that laid hands on Timothy (1 Tim 4:14) pointing towards a formal group.

It is virtually impossible to determine what the relationship is between the *episkopos* and *presbyteroi* in the Christian church but the role of the *presbyteroi* in Judiasm is better known. They were not the synagogue leaders[80] rather in the gospels it is used of the elders of the people. Jerusalem, like the Greek cities had been governed by a council "elderly, experienced and wise senior citizens called the *gerousia* (Pietersen 1994, 109). We know this council as the Sanhedrin but this same group is referred to in Josephus as the *presbyteroi*. In Judaism these men were the community leaders and if anything were the ones that appointed the synagogue officials (Pietersen 1994, 110). As the Christian community grew and developed a distinctly different identity, a possible role of the *presbyteroi* is as a governing council, just as the Jews would have had a governing council. (Pietersen 1994,

---

[80] The synagogue leader was the archisynagogos and the person who did the practical jobs in the church was the diakonos (Pietersen 1994, 110)

110)

Relation of Episkopos and Presbyteroi to Poimēn

Episcpos is only used in connection with Gentile churches, It has been suggested that episcopos is simply a gentile term for leaders of gentile churches and presbyteroi is primarily the Jewish term for the same office (Mappes 1997, 164). The terms can be used interchangeably as seen in Acts 20:17. Paul summoned the *presbyteros* (plural) of the Ephesian church (singular) to Miletus. There he told them that God has appointed them as *episkopos*. While elder and overseer are interchangeable, Fee believes that it does not exhaust the meaning of the word elder. He suggests elders is a covering term for both overseers and deacons (1985, 142).

Outside the Pastorals, the word episcopos or overseer appears in Acts 20:28; Phil 1:11; and 1 Pet. 2:25. In 1 Peter it refers to Jesus Christ as the church's guardian but in the other books it appears to be a title of a church officer as in 1 Timothy. The other officer from the Pastoral the *presbyteroi* or elder is also used widely in other New Testament books. A tile for church office that we are very familiar with, *poimēn* translated shepherd or pastor, is not found in the Pastorals. It is used seven times of Jesus who is the great shepherd (John 10:2, 11, 12, 14, 16; Heb. 13:20; 1 Pet. 2:25). It is used only once in Eph 4:11 for a local church ruler but the verb *poimainō* is used four times to describe the elders who are to feed the church (John 21:6; Acts 20:28; 1 Cor 9:7; 1 Pet 5:2). Paul wrote to Titus about the appointing *presbyteroi* and gave him the necessary qualifications(1:5-9). In the midst of these qualifications the same person is called an *episkopos* (1:6) (singular). Without any change of subject there is no reason to believe Paul has changed from speaking about elders to bishops. In Philippians 1:1 Paul refers to the church leaders as episcopos and *diakonoi* with no mention of *presbyteroi*. If it is claimed that *episcopos* and *presbyteroi* are identifiably different, then good grounds need to be given for Paul excluding one of the church's important office bearers. The same linking of roles is found in 1 Peter 5:1-12 where both officers are exercising oversight.

Further support for identifying the two offices can be found in Acts 20:28 where the terms are used interchangeably of an office while the shepherding describes their function of protecting, guiding and feeding the sheep. The same is seen in 1 Peter 5:2. These associations strengthen the linking of teacher to pastor in Eph 4:11 as one office with the twofold function of overseeing the flock and teaching it. This linking of terms removes the validity of the Episcopal system. Mappes summarises the titles saying "the three terms πρεσβύτερος, ἐπίσκοπος, and ποιμήν are different names for those who occupy the same office. The πρεσβύτερος stresses godly wisdom and maturity, ἐπίσκοπος points to oversight and rule, while ποιμήν points to feeding and tending the flock".

There were two areas of ministry involved giving oversight and teaching/preaching and it has been suggested that there were two officers involved, i.e. teaching and ruling elders. This was promoted by Calvin based on 1 Timothy 5:17 which says "Let the elders who rule well be considered worthy of double honour, especially those who labour in preaching and teaching". Further support is claimed from 1 Cor. 12:28; and the lack of teaching as a qualification as a qualification in 1 Tim. 3:1-7. It is far from certain however that that the different functions of eldership did not require separate individuals to fill them. Paul was an apostle but also called himself a preacher and a teacher (I Tim. 2:7; 2 Tim. 1:11) an intermingling of gifts and offices (Mounce 1997, 172). The Corinthian passage also mixes gifts with offices. The strongest support comes from 1 Tim. 5:17 but, are the elders that rule different to those who labour in the difficult task of preaching and teaching? There are several teaching elders, not one, these teachers also rule but it does not follow that all ruling elders regularly teach and preach. While not all ruling elders may not have had the gifts of teaching and preaching it is a requirement of their office that they can teach, and teach accurately, when needed. This is a distinction of function rather than office.

The Diakonoi

The qualifications for the *diakonoi* are very similar to those of the *episkopos*, dealing not with what he does but what he is, i.e. moral qualities. While the *diakonoi* can be seen as fulfilling the roll of the servant within the household of God it sells the role very short to see him just as a servant. Those who perform this role well had a very high standing in the community and their ministry built up their confidence in the faith (1 Tim. 3:13). Paul was pleased to use this word and also *dulos*, slave to describe himself (Rom. 1;1; Phil. 1;1) and used both words of Timothy (1 Tim 4:6).

The qualifications for the deacons are only marginally if actually inferior to those of the overseer and elder. While eldership is a spirit energised ministry with or without formal appointment (Mappes 1997, 170) it is also a function with set roles such as teaching. We know that some of the seven good men in Acts 6:3

who's official role was the administering the charity of the church had powerful preaching and evangelistic skills. This was function without office.

Paul had said "The saying is sure:[81] whoever aspires to the office of bishop desires a noble task "(1 Tim. 3:1). The qualifications for elders required that they be proved blameless and faithful in the Christian community and this means "some level of prior ministry or function is required for eldership" (Mappes 1997, 171). Paul's case in all offices is that competency in a lesser function is evidence of how the person will operate in the greater office. This function starts in the management of their home and person, and extends to the ministry of the church. "If one does not function effectively without office, how can he function effectively in office?" (Mappes 1997, 171). In this manner the office of deacon can be viewed as an apprenticeship for eldership where evidence of function can be seen. It is a place where the training for an exemplary life can begin.

With the troubles in the church arising from elders it is not surprising that as much care is taken in the appointment of deacons as it is of elders. These men (and women?) were the future of the church and is a reminder that ministry is concerned with generations, not months or years.

The Role of Women

---

[81] Some interpreters place these words at the end of the previous paragraph. Other ancient authorities read The saying is commonly accepted

Spencer states the problem of women's ministry clearly when she says "First Timothy seems inconsistent with the contemporary achievements of women or the concept of a loving God" (Spencer 1974, 216). It also seems inconsistent with the very impressive list of women who have worked in ministry with him in Romans 16. There, ten women are affirmed by Paul, two of these have been so involved in missionary work they have been imprisoned. Though the great number of those in the evangelical tradition following the restrictive historical view (Hughes 1999, 102), is it possible to hold a more liberal view arguing on the "basis of the accepted exegetical methodology" (Moo 1981, 199)?

The qualifications are "rather general and unexceptional" and "most of them are virtues which every believer, female and male, minister and layman, should possess" (Moo 1981, 212). Actually the table of elder qualifications show that the exact same requirements are expected of women as for the overseer. It seems very unfair to demand standards of all women, even young widows and most men do not posses and yet say that when they achieve it there is not the same outlet for this maturity and knowledge as for men. How is this fundamentally different to the cast system that says it is better for a man to be working poorly in his cast than a person do the task well outside of his cast.

Paul at no time deals comprehensively with women in ministry. Stiefel claims most evidence for woman's ministry is indirect. He refers to Pliny torturing two female slaves and commentating that they were *ministrae* (possibly *diakonos*) (1995, 457). In 1 Tim 3:11 the reference to women is also incidental. Reference has already been made to Phoebe the female deacon[82] from Cenchreae (just outside Corinth) mentioned in the greetings in Chapter 16 of Romans. Even a critic of women teaching such as Moo begrudgingly admits that there is no doubt that phoebe was some sort of minister at Cenchrea (1981, 210). It is entirely possible that our book of Romans is actually a copy that was sent to Ephesus (Koester 1995, 123) which would mean that in churches Paul founded and/or organized, women had leadership roles. Paul even refers to Junia who was outstanding among the apostles[83]; Junia was a common Roman female name (Payne 1981, 184). We also know of Euodia and Syntyche who "have struggled beside me in the work of the gospel" (Phil 4:2-3).

The New Testament terms describing the activities of these women are terms normally associated with leadership positions: "explaining the way of God more accurately" (Acts 18:26), "deacon" (Rom 16:1), "ruler" (Rom 16:2), "my fellow worker in Christ Jesus" (Rom 16:3; Phil 4:3), "apostle" (Rom 16:7), "worked hard in the Lord" (Rom 16:6, 12), and "contended at my side in the cause of the gospel" (Phil 4:3). "If women are represented in the New Testament as fulfilling functions known to be associated with leadership positions, it is reasonable to assume that they were in fact appointed to the offices associated with such activities "

---

[82] There is no female form of deacon in the New Testament (Payne 1981, 194). The word is frequently translated as servant avoiding the problem despite using minister or deacon in other occurrences of the word, especially when προστάτις implies official ruling (Payne 1981, 196). Kittle agrees also (G. Kittel, G. W. Bromiley & G. Friedrich, Ed. 1964-c1976, G2003). Moo argues strongly that we cannot be sure that it was a fully fledged deacon, probably a helper or protector but possibly an administrator of charitable work (1981, 210). But this role in Acts was a male only prerogative (Acts 6:1-6) so there is at minimum a significant shift towards women.

[83] Moo is probably correct that she is a small "a" apostle as opposed to a capital "A" Apostle who has seen Christ (Moo 1981, 209). But she is a messenger none the less with an authority apparently exceeding that of an overseer.

(Payne 1981, 197).

The New Testament church was built on the foundation of the apostles and prophets[84] (Eph. 2:20). Philip's four daughters were all prophets (Acts 21:9 see also Anna in Luke 2:26-38, daughters in Acts 2:17.) Paul just assumes that women will be prophesying in the assembly in Corinth (1 Cor. 11:5).

This should not surprise us. Paul was so comfortable with his friends Priscilla and Aquilla that he was in secular business with and shared ministry with them. Priscilla is mentioned frequently before Aquilla, which was very uncommon. She must have had a strong personality and great ability for this to occur and Paul calls her his fellow worker in Christ Jesus (Rom. 16:3-5). Priscilla and her husband taught[85] Appollos, a man and a teacher of men and Acts records this without any unfavourable comment. If the teaching role of Priscilla was incorrect then Paul was a hypocrite. The indirect evidence is strongly in favour of women taking a leadership role in the church at least at the level of Deacon and their functional role may well have been greater than their office.

---

[84] Attempts to see the prophets role as inferior to that of the teacher are put aside by Eph. 3:5 where "which in other generations was not made known to the sons of men, as it has now been made known to the sons of men, as it has now been revealed to his holy apostles and prophets in the spirit." In 1 Cor. 12:28 teaching is ranked after prophets. See also Acts 13:1.

[85] Moo seems to be clutching at straws when he maintains Priscilla did not teach anyone, she merely instructed Apollos (1981, 202) Hughes who takes a similar viewpoint on women's ministry says it was teaching (1999, 108). Moo understands teaching as "involving the careful transmission of Christian tradition and the authoritative proclamation of God's will based on that tradition and study of scriptures" which is generally the contemporary understanding (1981, 207). He also believes that the expression teach is narrower than our present usage but does not define it (1981, 202). This is not helpful when the word is applied widely in a contemporary setting to restrict women's ministry.

Their function, if not their office allowed them to work hard In the Lord and win the respect of the Apostle (Rom. 16:1–3, 6, 12, 13, 15) and in the case of Priscilla fulfilled the role of an *episcopos*. Any ban seems to be related to the city and the circumstances than a blanket authoritative statement. In the same time frame "Phoebe had been praised in her position of authority while the women at Ephesus had been restrained" (Spencer 1974, 221).

The Pastorals, along with the indirect evidence show a role for women advanced generally for its time but not especially advanced for Ephesus. Women in Asia Minor were more conspicuous in religious life than elsewhere (Strelan 1994, 120). They served an important role[86] in the religious life of Ephesus sometimes even serving as priests. This would be expected following the role of the Amazons in founding the worship of Artemis Ephesia (Pausanius, History of Greece, 7.2.4). A number of these women were known to have held this office in their own right, not being dependant on their husbands (Friesen U.D., 84-86, Strelan 1994, 120). They were actually involved in the sacrificial activities from c. 45 A.D. (Friesen U.D., 113). Women also served as priestesses in the Artemisia and in the cult of Hestia Boulaia in the civic centre. In the Imperial cult, 26% of the 138 known high priests were women (Koester 1995, 58). This prominent role would not be un-noticed by Ephesian Jews and Christians.

The suppression of women's ministry can be argued from the Greek culture of the day (Barclay 1975, 77-78). But a book that

---

[86] In Asia Minor, 28 women are known to have held the position of *pyrtanis* (a position of very high rank involving the finances and cultic life of the city) in eight cities in the first three centuries of the Common Era; 37 were *stephanephoroi* (positions of high public profile and prestige, if not much political clout) in 17 cities over a five century period; and 18 women in 14 different cities held the position of *agonothetis* (a position of responsibility for contests) in the first three centuries. (Trebilco 1991, 120-122).

simply reflects cultural values at a given time cannot be authoritative (see comments on authority and inspiration earlier). How much of scripture could be put on this argument (Spencer 1974, 216). Paul's own teaching also seems to be contradictory to this ban. Christ has made us one, breaking down the dividing walls (Eph. 2:14). There is no longer any division between groups of people but only whether they are in Christ (Col. 3:1) extending even to the division of male and female (Gal 3:28).

It is possible however that there were women *diakonoi* as 1 Tim 3:11 in the passage dealing with the qualifications (verses 8-13) refers to women and requiring the same qualifications of them. They are to be serious or worthy of honour, at a time when not a great deal of honour was given to women. The same adjective is used of men in 3:8. Also they are not to be slanderers which is the charge given to the older women in 2 Tim. 3:2-3. Similar to the charge to the male *diakonoi* to hold fast to the mystery of the faith (1 Tim. 3:9) the women were to be faithful or trustworthy in everything. While these may have only been the wives of the *diakonoi* the sense of the passage suggests not. The qualities are not gender specific and in no way differentiated from those of men. More compellingly, Paul refers to Phoebe as a *diakonos* (Rom 16:1). Had Paul not mentioned her name and role we would not have evidence of an actual woman serving in this role usually considered the task of men

The word 'likewise' reflects 3:8 where it signals the beginning of a new topic and here we would also be expecting to see a new group which relates to the previous two. The plural noun for woman has no definite article. This suggests three possible interpretations about who these women were. Possibly it is an anarthrous noun used as general reference to all women but this means that the high requirements for just some men were imposed on all women (Stiefel 1995, 445). This is unreasonable. Alternatively terms of relationship when spoken of in general do not need the article (Stiefel 1995, 446). This would make the women in a relationship with the male deacons i.e. their wives. This is the traditional view but working against this is that there are no requirements for the wife of the *episkopos*. A third possibility is again that it is an anarthrous noun to specify a counterpart with the "appropriate occupational term implied but unexpressed, that is intending something like "women (ones) likewise" (Stiefel 1995, 447). Stiefel refers to this as being the more widely accepted understanding (Stiefel 1995, 453).

What was the role of thee women? Roles for women diakonoi suggested by Pietersen are waiting on tables and assisting at the baptism of women (1994, 114). This menial role seems inadequate for people with such high morals and character. They do not have a separate name to the male *diakonoi* and this may well be because they were not a separate group but included among the *diakonoi*.

Though they may have prophesied, neither the male nor the female diakonos are seen as teaching which is the role of the episkopos. The Pastorals (1 Tim. 2:9-12) and I Corinthians 14:34-35 does show reservations about women teaching men? While the verses are similar, the settings are very different; Paul had problems with particular women in particular churches. In Corinth the women, along with the tongue speakers and prophets were disrupting the meetings. In the Pastorals the emphasis is on peace and quiet while learning (Padgett 1987, 24) opposed to the disruption of the heretics. The word *manthano* implies structured learning. While this indicates that the women were recent converts we must weigh fully the fact that the women were being instructed at all. Female god fearers and Jews were excluded from instruction in the scriptures in the synagogues[87] (Padgett 1987, 24). The women had already submitted themselves to the false teachers and unknowingly, even to Satan (1 Tim 1:3-7; 4:1). Instead these women should now submit to those who teach the words of faith 1 Tim. 4:6. Rather than never teach, they were to learn properly (Payne 1981, 178). Learning[88] in silence was not an imposition on women who had been too vocal in spreading false teaching but an invitation to learn as the men did. Simon, the son of Gamaliel, Paul's teacher said

> All my days I grew up among the sages, and I have found nothing better for a person than silence. Study is not the most important thing, but deed: whosoever indulges in too many words brings about sin (Mishnah 17, Aboth)

It is remarkable that Gamaliel's zealous student Paul should have

---

87 "Although there are some references to Jewish women knowing the law such as b. Erub. 53b–54a, b. Ketub. 23a, y. Sabb. 6, 1 and y. Sota 3:4; the more common attitude is reflected in the words of Rabbi Eliezer (c. AD 90), "If a man gives his daughter a knowledge of the law it is as though he taught her extravagance" (rn. Sota 3:4, cf. b. Sota 2lb) and in y. Sota 8 and 10a, "May the words of the Torah be burned rather than be handed over to women." Women were forbidden to teach (rn. Qidd. 4:13) and were not required to perform the religious rituals for the annual feasts.[24] Their position in society is reflected in the common formula, "women, slaves, and children" (rn. Ber. 3:3; m. Sukk. 2:8; m. Ros. Has. 1:8; m.B. Mes. 1:5). In the home, too, the wife was not even to pronounce the benediction after a meal (m. Ber. 7:2) "(Payne 1981, 188).

88 "If [women's] susceptibility to deception was that severe we would have expected Paul to bar them from being taught following the common practice in synagogues at that time (Payne 1981, 178).

moved to a position so contrary to Jewish practice at the time. But there was really nothing new in this as during the exodus and conquest, women, not just men were urged to attend the reading of the Law (Deut 31:12; Josh 8:35). Sadly though, by the first century women were exempted from learning the law so she could concentrate on being a home maker (Spencer 1974, 218). The best a woman could hope for would be to hear (as opposed to learning) from the back lobby and have no part of the synagogue service. With Mary and Martha, Jesus had encouraged such learning taking precedence over household duties (Luke 10:38-42). For many woman learning in silence would lead to a situation where they would have at least the ability to become authoritative teachers" (Spencer 1974, 220). Did Paul intend woman to always remain at the early stage of growth as we see in Ephesus or should they reach their potential.

Very dogmatic statements about the role of women in ministry are made from 1 Timothy 2:11-15 This is "a difficult passage, containing unusual vocabulary (αὐθεντέω, ἡσυχία), awkward grammar (the link between vv. 14 and 15), references to the Old Testament (Gen 2 and 3) whose New Testament usage needs to be determined in 1 Timothy 2:13–14, significant theological issues (e.g., the use of σῴζω), and a flow of thought that is not so clear as it may seem at first glance (Bowman 1992, 194). Extra to this list can be added a church situation which is poorly understood and a modern church with teaching opportunities never envisaged in the first century.

Kent is typical of those who limit the role of women. He sees no public outlet for what they have learned, basing his argument on the meaning of *didaskein* in 1 Tim. 2:12, which is the present, meaning to be a teacher, not the aorist, meaning to teach. Despite these same people becoming the judges of the world and angels (6:2-3) he believes this precludes women from being the authoritative bearers of doctrine (Kent 1958, 113). The significance of the word is accepted but not the conclusion as he misses the significance of the context. Paul does not have in mind a permanent ban on women teachers (Payne 1981, 172) but just these women as he uses epitrepo the first person present, not the aorist (Padgett 1987, 25; Spencer 1974, 220)[89]. When properly instructed there was no reason for them not to serve as deacons (Padgett 1987, 25).

The existence of female diakonoi does not mean that their role was the same as the men. Using the model of the church being the family of God it would require the woman, like the wife, to have "status and religious obligations" (Pietersen 1994, 114). It is suggested that family model of the church would have pressured the women to concentrate their ministries in the domestic arena and so vanish from the scene as a distinct group (Stiefel 1995, 456). While it may explain, it does not justify a diminished role.

Paul had shown that he was willing to compromise on peripheral

---

[89] "Paul could have written, "I will never permit ..." using the future tense, as is done in Matt 26:33, "I will never be offended"; or he could have used the subjunctive, as occurs twice in Heb 13:5, "I will never leave you nor forsake you." A formulation like either of these would have indicated a continuing prohibition, but Paul gave no indication that 1 Tim 2:12 should be understood as a continuing prohibition." (Payne 1981, ???). Moo who disagrees with women teaching men agrees that the verb is used fourteen out of eighteen times for "temporarily limited situations' But cites Rom 12:1 "I am beseeching you, brothers, to offer your bodies as living sacrifices (Moo 1981, 200-1). There seems a big gulf between accepting a call to holiness as universal and accepting what could be a repressive social situation as a divinely inspired norm.

issues such as the time he circumcised Timothy to keep harmony with the Jews Acts 16:13. It is quite possible that as church settled in for the long haul and with the passing of the apostles and men like Timothy and Titus that the eschatological fervour of the original message began to wane. Ehrman suggests that "the Roman ideology of gender relationships became Christianised and the social implications of Paul's apocalyptic vision became lost (1997, 350). Hughes argues that "the revisionist" view only coincides with the feminist movement with the first paper occurring in 1969 followed by a flood of articles (1999, 103). He argues that by rejecting 1900 years of tradition we are accepting the spirit of the age when it should be resisted (1999 104). It is better to argue that for 1900 years the male leaders of the church did not resist the spirit of their age[90]. Those who seek the teaching role of women must much clearer scriptural evidence[91] as so much hinges on verses that do not "constitute clear evidence" (Moo 1981, 201).

The Widows

In the New Testament environment, women were dependant legally and financially initially on their parents and then their husbands. With the much shorter life span, the issues of widows was more acute and wives could become widows at a very early age. Charity towards widows has been a hallmark of both Judaism and Christianity (James 1:27). In the Pastorals the duty towards them is recognized but some, it appears, were expecting

---

[90] Perhaps the Puritans were right when they said, "There is yet more light and truth to break forth from His word"

[91] Traditional scholars say that it the revisionists that have to prove their case (Moo 1981, 196 & 209, Hughes 1999, 103). I believe the minimum the revisionists have to establish is reasonable doubt based on unclear texts.

the church to take care of widows that they themselves had a family responsibility to help. Financially the church should only have been concerned with those who needed help and there was a responsibility on behalf of the widow to "receive it responsibly, setting an example of faith and piety" (Pietersen 1994, 117).

There was a list of enrolled widows who were to receive the charity of the church but only the elderly could be added to it. Young women are to be excluded as they will be distracted and remarry forsaking their commitment which appears to be a vow of celibacy.[92] It was better for the young to remarry 1 Cor. 7:9. There was a danger that the young women would be idle, visiting homes and spreading gossip (Verses 11-12) This visitation could also be associated with spreading unorthodox teaching and keeping alive old wives tales (1 Tim. 4:7) as seen in the Acts of Paul. These younger widows, through no fault of their own, would usually have little if any formal education and now without their husbands were devoid of any guidance. From the exclusions some take the enrolled widows as a ministry order in the church with duties of prayer intercession and visitation. Others see this not as an order but as a list of those entitled to the charity of the church (Pietersen 1994, 117) but that with the privilege came the responsibility to pray for the rich (Pietersen 1994, 116).

The structure of 1 Timothy 3 supports the idea that a social group, not an office is in mind as the reference to the enrolled widows is not in the section dealing with the character of the office holders. The section addresses the older and younger women and finishes with the slaves. There is reference to presbyters here also but they

---

[92] The suggestion by Pietersen (1994, 119) that this was a commitment to be espoused to Christ seems to go too far

may not be "so much "officers" as respected wise men of the community, who like the real widows, receive a "pension" from the church" (Pietersen 1994, 120).

9 WORKS CITED

_____ The Didache in Kraft Robert A. *The Apostolic Fathers Vol. III*. Thomas Nelson and Son, Toronto and New York, 1965.

_____ The Acts of Paul and Thecla in *Anthology of Ancient Greek Popular Literature* Edited by William Hansen and translated by R. McL. Wilson. Bloomington and Indianapolis: Indiana University Press, 1998.

Arnold, Clinton E. *Ephesians: Power and Magic, The Concept of Power in Ephesians in Light of its Historical Setting.* Cambridge New York and Sydney: Cambridge, University Press, 1989.

Barclay, William. *Ambassador for Christ*. Edinbrough: St. Andrew Press, 1973.

Barclay, William. *A Plain Man Looks at the Lord's Prayer*. Collins: Glasgow 1964.

Barclay, William. *Ethics in a Permissive Society*. London : Fontana, 1971

Barclay, William. *The Letters to Timothy, Titus, and Philemon.* Sydney: Christian Press Australia 1987.

Boring M. E., K. Berger, and C. Colpe, *Hellenistic Commentary to the New Testament* (Nashville: Abingdon, 1995).

Brown, Raymond E., *The Gospel According to John I-XII*, Anchor Bible Series Vol. 29. New York: Doubleday, 1966.

Brown, Raymond E., *An Introduction to the New Testament*. New York: Doubleday, 1997.

Bruce, F.F. *The Spreading Flame* Eerdmans: Grand Rapids, 1992 (reprint)

Bultmann, Rudolph. Gnosis in *Theological Dictionary of the New Testament*. ed. G. Kittel, G. W. Bromiley & G. Friedrich. Eerdmans: Grand Rapids, 1964, 689-719.

Carson D.A, Douglas J. Moo, & Leon Morris, *An introduction to the New Testament*, Leicester: APOLLOS, 1992.

Clement First Epistle to the Corinthians in Roberts, A., Donaldson, J., & Coxe, A. C. 1997. *The Ante-Nicene Fathers Vol.I* : Translations of the writings of the Fathers down to A.D. 325. The apostolic fathers with Justin Martyr and Irenaeus. Logos Research Systems: Oak Harbor

Clement. First Epistle in Roberts, A., Donaldson, J., & Coxe, A. C. 1997. *The Ante-Nicene Fathers Vol. VIII* : Translations of the writings of the Fathers down to A.D. 325. Fathers of the Third and Fourth Centuries: The Twelve Patriarchs, Excerpts and Epistles, The Clementina, Apocrypha, Decretals, Memoirs of Edessa and Syriac Documents, Remains of the First Ages. Logos Research Systems: Oak Harbor.

De Welt, Don. *Paul's Letters to Timothy and Titus*. Joplin: College Press, 1981

Dibelius, Martin, Hans Conzelmann. *The Pastoral Epistles*. Philadelphia: Fortress Press, 1972.

Dunn, James D.G. The First and Second Letters to Timothy and the Letter to Titus in *The New Interpreters Bible* Vol. X1 ed. Leander E. Keck et. al. 775-880. Nashville: Abingdon, 2000

Ehrman, Bart D., The New Testament: A Historical Introduction to the Early Christian Writings. New York: Oxford, 1997. Quoted in Mappes David A. "Moral Virtues Associated with Eldership" Bibliotheca Sacra Volume 160 (2003) 203-219

Elwell, Walter A. *Encountering the New Testament*. Grand Rapids: Baker 1997.

Eusebius. Ecclesiastical History in Schaff, P. *The Nicene and Post-Nicene Fathers Second Series Vol. I.* Eusebius: Church History, Life of Constantine the Great, and Oration in Praise of Constantine. Logos Research Systems: Oak Harbor,1997.

Fee, Gordon D. *Corinthians, a Study Guide*. Brussels: ICI, 1979.

Fee, Gordon D, D Stuart, *How to Read the Bible for all its Worth*. Grand Rapids: Zondervan, 1982.

Fee, Gordon D. The First Epistle to the Corinthians. Grand Rapids: Eerdmans, 1987.

Fee, Gordon D. *1 and 2 Timothy, Titus.* Peabody: Hendrickson Publishers Inc., 1995

Friesen, Steven J. *Twice Neokoros Ephesus, Asia and the Cult of the Flavian Imperial Policy, Religions in the Graeco-Roman World* Volume 116. Leiden and New York: E.J. Brill, U.D.

Gealy, F.D. *The First and Second Epistles to Timothy and Titus* in The Interpreters Bible. New York: Abingdon, 1955

Goodspeed, E.J. The Place of Ephesus in Early Christian Literature: New Chapters in New Testament Study. New

York, 1937. Quoted in Eugene E. Lemcio *"Ephesus and the New Testament Canon",* John Rylands University Library of Manchester 69 (1986-7): 210-234.

Gordon, Alan, "James: Diatribe, Paraenesis or Protreptic Discourse? The Hellenistic Subgenre of the Letter of James". Dr. Th. Diss., Australian College of Theology, 2002.

Gritz, Sharon H. *Paul, Women Teachers and the Mother Goddess at Ephesus.* Lanham: University Press of America, 1991.

Gunther, John J. *St. Paul's Opponents and their Background: A study of Apocalyptic and Jewish Sectarian Teaching.* Leiden: E.J. Brill, 1973

Guthrie, Donald, *The Pastoral Epistles*, Grand Rapids: Wm. B. Eerdmans Publishing Co., 1957.

Guthrie, Donald, *New Testament Introduction* Downers Grove: Intervarsity Press, 1990.

Guy H.A. *The Gospel of Mark.* Basingstoke and London: Macmillan Education Limited, 1968.

Harland, Philip A. *Honours and Worship: Emperors, Imperial Cults and Associations at Ephesus (first to third centuries c.e.)* Studies in Religion / Sciences religieuses 25 (1996) 319-34. Reprinted http://www.philipharland.com/articleSR.htm by permission of the Canadian Corporation for Studies in Religion.

Harris, R. L., Archer, G. L., & Waltke, B. K. *Theological Wordbook of the Old Testament* (electronic ed.). Moody Press: Chicago1999, c1980

Hiebert, Edmond. *First Timothy*. Chicago: Moody Press, 1957.

Hendriksen, W. *1&2 Thessalonians, 1&2 Timothy & Titus*. Edinburgh: Banner of Truth, 1983.

Howe, E. Margaret. "The Positive Case for the Ordination of Women," Perspectives in Evangelical Theology, ed. K. Kantzer and S. Gundry (Grand Rapids: Baker, 1979) 276 in Philip B Payne. *"Liberterian Women in Ephesus: A Response to Douglas J. Moo's Article, "1 Timothy 2:11-15: Meaning and Signifigance".*" Trinity Journal Volume 2 (1981) 170-198

Ignatius UD Epistle to the Magnesians in Roberts, A., Donaldson, J., & Coxe, A. C. 1997. *The Ante-Nicene Fathers Vol. I* : Translations of the writings of the Fathers down to A.D. 325. The apostolic fathers with Justin Martyr and Irenaeus. Logos Research Systems: Oak Harbor

Ignatius UD Epistle to the Smyrnaeans in Roberts, A., Donaldson, J., & Coxe, A. C. 1997. *The Ante-Nicene Fathers Vol. I* : Translations of the writings of the Fathers down to A.D. 325. The apostolic fathers with Justin Martyr and Irenaeus. Logos Research Systems: Oak Harbor

Ignatius UD Epistle to the Trallains in Roberts, A., Donaldson, J., & Coxe, A. C. 1997. *The Ante-Nicene Fathers Vol..I* : Translations of the writings of the Fathers down to A.D. 325. The apostolic fathers with Justin Martyr and Irenaeus. Logos Research Systems: Oak Harbor.

Isocrates. *Isocrates with an English Translation in three volumes*, by George Norlin. London: William Heinemann Ltd. 1980.

Johnson, Luke Timothy. *The First and Second Letters to Timothy* (New York: Doubleday, 2001)

Josephus, Flavius *Complete Works* translated William Whinston. London: Pickering and Inglis Ltd, 1960.

Karris, Robert J, *Pastoral Epistles (New Testament Message 17 : a Biblical-Theological Commentarty)* 1973

Kelly, J.N.D. *Commentary on the Pastoral Epistles.* Grand Rapids: Barker, 1981.

Kittel, G., Friedrich, G., & Bromiley, G. W. 1995, c1985. *Theological Dictionary of the New Testament.* Translation of: Theologisches Worterbuch zum Neuen Testament. W.B. Eerdmans: Grand Rapids, Mich.

Kendal R.T. *Westminster Record* Oct 1984

Kent Homer A. *The Pastoral Epistles.* Chicago: Moody Press, 1958

Koester, Helmut. *Introduction to the New Testament: History and Literature of early Christianity.* Philadelphia: Fortress Press, 1982.

Koester, Helmut. Ed. *Ephesos, Metropolis of Asia.* Valley Forge: Harvard Theological Studies, 1995. Papers presented at a symposium organised by Harvard Divinity School and co sponsored by Harvard University Departments of Classics and fine Arts March 1994

Lenski, R.C.H. *The Interpretation of St. Paul's Epistles to the Colossians, to the Thessalonians, to Timothy, to Titus, and to Philemon.* Minneapolis: Arzburg Publishing House 1964 (reprint).

Lock Walter. *The Pastoral Epistles*. Edinbrough: T &T Clark, 1978.

Louisiana Baptist University and Theological Seminary, 2000-2001 Catalogue. Shreveport: 2000.

Marshall I. Howard. *The Pastoral Epistles*, International Critical Commentary, ed J.A. Emertonm C.E.B. Cranfield, and G.N Stanton. London: T&T Clark, 1999.

Mishnah 17, Aboth in Aida Dina Besancon Spencer. "Eve at Ephesus (Should Women Be Ordained As Pastors According To The First Letter To Timothy 2:11-15)." JETS Volume 17::4 (1974) 220-230.

Mounce, William D. *Pastoral Epistles*. Nashville: Thomas Nelson Publishers, 2000.

Oldfather, William A, "Introduction," in Aeneas Tacticus, Asclepiodotus, Onasander, in Loeb Classical Library. Cambridge, MA: Harvard University Press, 1923,

Onasander in *Aeneas Tacticus, Asclepiodotus, Onasander*, in Loeb Classical Library. Cambridge, MA: Harvard University Press, 1923,

Pausanius. *Description of Greece*, Translated by J.G. Frazer, Loeb Classical Library. New York: Biblo and Tannen 1965 6 volumes 1918-35.

Pietersen, Lloyd K. *The Polemic of the Pastorals*. London & New York: T&T Clark International, 1994.

Pliny the Elder. *The Natural History*. ed. John Bostock, M.D., F.R.S., H.T. Riley, Esq., Digital Library Project. [online] URL http://www.perseus.tufts.edu .Ed. Gregory R.

Crane. updated 12 April 2006. Tufts University. [accessed 30 November 2008]

Philo. *De Vita Mosis II*, in The Works of Philo Judaeus, the contemporary of Josephus, translated by Charles Duke Yonge. London: H. G. Bohn, 1854.

Polybius. *Histories*. ed. Evelyn S. Shuckburgh. translator. London, New York. Macmillan. 1889. Reprint Bloomington 1962. Digital Library Project. [online] URL http://www.perseus.tufts.edu .Ed. Gregory R. Crane. updated 12 April 2006. Tufts University. [accessed 25 October 2010]

Polycarp Epistle to the Philippians in Roberts, A., Donaldson, J., & Coxe, A. C. 1997. *The Ante-Nicene Fathers Vol.I* : Translations of the writings of the Fathers down to A.D. 325. The apostolic fathers with Justin Martyr and Irenaeus. Logos Research Systems: Oak Harbor, 1997,

Stevenson, J. *A New Eusebius*. London: SPCK, 1957

Strelan, Rick. "Paul, Artemis, and the Jews." Ph.D. Diss., University of Queensland, 1994.

T.G.T. in introduction to Luthers Works Volume 54: Table Talk, ed Jaroslav Jan Pelikan, Hilton C. Oswald and Helmut T Lehmann Philadelphia: Fortress Press, 1999, c1967 electronic edition

Tenny, M. *New Testament Survey*. London: IVP, 1973.

Tertullian Against Marcion in Roberts, A., Donaldson, J., & Coxe, A. C.. *The Ante-Nicene Fathers Vol. III* : Translations of the writings of the Fathers down to A.D. 325. Latin Christianity: Its Founder, Tertullian. Logos Research Systems: Oak Harbor,1997.

Tertullian, On Baptism in Roberts, A., Donaldson, J., & Coxe, A. C.. *The Ante-Nicene Fathers Vol. III* : Translations of the writings of the Fathers down to A.D. 325. Latin Christianity: Its Founder, Tertullian. Logos Research Systems: Oak Harbor, 1997.

Thielicke, Helmut. *Ethics of Sex* Trans. by John W. Doberstein. New York, Evanston and London: Harper & Row, 1964.

Trebilco, Paul. *The Early Christians in Ephesus from Paul to Ignatius*. Wissenschaftliche Untersuchungen zum Neuen Testament, ed. Jörg Frey, vol 166. Tübingen: Mohr Siebeck, 2004.

Van Campenhausen, Hans. *Ecclesiastical Authority and Spiritual Power* translated J.A. Baker. Stanford: Stanford University Press, 1969.

Van Groningen, Gerard. *First Century Gnosticism: Its Origin and Motifs*. E.J. Brill: Leiden, 1967.

Wilson, Stephen G. *Luke and the Pastoral Epistles*. London: SPCK, 1979.

Xenophon of Ephesus. An Ephesian Tale in *Anthology of Ancient Greek Popular Literature* Edited by William Hansen and translated by Moses Hadas. Bloomington and Indianapolis: Indiana University Press, 1998.

Young, Frances *The Theology of the Pastoral Letters*. Cambridge: Cambridge University Press, 1994.

Zodhiates, S. 2000, c1992, c1993. *The Complete Word Study Dictionary : New Testament* (electronic ed.). AMG Publishers: Chattanooga, TN

Journals

Bowman, Ann L. "Women in Ministry: An Exergetical Study of 1 Timothy 2:11-15." Bibliotheca Sacra Volume 149 (1992) 194-214.

Brough, S.M. "The Apostle among the Amazons." Westminster Theological Journal 56 (1994): 154-172.

Baugh, Stephen M. "Savior of all People" Westminster Journal of Theology 54(1992) 331-40

Evans, Craig A. "Mark's Incipit and the Priene Calendar Inscription: From Jewish Gospel to Greco-Roman Gospel." Journal of Greco-Roman Christianity and Judaism 1 (2000) 67-81.

Fee, D. Gordon. "Reflections On Church Order In The Pastoral Epistles, With Further Reflections On The Hermeneutics of Ad Hoc Documents" JETS Volume 28 (1985) 142-152.

Fiore, Benjamin "Function of Personal Example in the Socratic and Pastoral Epistles" Analecta Biblica; 105 1986. XVIII-283.

Ford, J.M. "A Note on Proto-Montanism In The Pastoral Epistles", NTS 17 (1971) 338-346

Glasscock, Ed. "The Biblical Concept of Elder." Bibliotheca Sacra Volume144 (1987) 67-79.

Hay, David M. "Pistis as "Ground For Faith" in Hellenized Judaism And Paul" JBL 108 No 3 (1989), 461-476

Hughes R. Kent. "Living Out God's Order In The Church" MSJ Volume 10 (1999) 102-112.

Karris, Robert J. "The Background and Significance of the Polemic of the Pastoral Epistles." Journal of Biblical Literature 92 (1973) 549-564.

MacLeod, David J. "Christology in Six Lines: An Exposition of 1 Timothy 3:16" Bibliotheca Sacra Volume 159 (2002) 335-349

Mappes, David A. "The New Testament Elder, Overseer, and Pastor" Bibliotheca Sacra Volume 154 (1997) 163-175.

Mappes, David A. "The Discipline of a sinning Elder " Bibliotheca Sacra Volume 154 (1997) 334-334.

Mappes, David A. "The "Laying on of Hands" of Elders" Bibliotheca Sacra Volume 154 (1997) 457-497.

Mappes, David A. "The Heresy Paul Opposed in 1 Timothy" Bibliotheca Sacra Volume 156 (1999) 452-459..

Mappes, David A. "Moral Virtues Associated with Eldership" Bibliotheca Sacra Volume 160 (2003) 203-219

Moo, Douglas J. "The Interpretation of 1 Timothy 2:11-15: A Rejoinder." Trinity Journal, Volume 2 (1981)199-213

Moule, C.F.D. "The Problem of the Pastoral Epistles: A

Reappraisal", Buletin of the John Rylands Library 1965 430-452

Padgett, Alan. "Wealthy Women at Ephesus 1 Timothy 2:8-15 in Social Context." Interpretation Volume XLmenI (1987) 19-31.

Payne Philip B. "Liberterian Women in Ephesus: A Response to Douglas J. Moo's Article, "1 Timothy 2:11-15: Meaning and Signifigance"." Trinity Journal Volume 2 (1981) 170-198

Saucy, Robert L. "The Husband of One Wife" Bibliotheca Sacra Volume 131 (1974) 230-242

Saucy, Robert L. "Womens Prohibition To Teach Men: An Investigation Into Its Meaning And Contemporary Application." JETS Volume 37:1 (1994) 80-99.

Spencer, Aida Dina Besancon. "Eve at Ephesus (Should Women Be Ordained As Pastors According To The First Letter To Timothy 2:11-15)." JETS Volume 17::4 (1974) 220-230.

Stiefel, Jennifer H. Women Deacons in 1 Timothy: A linguistic and Literary Look at "women Likewise . . ." (1 Tim 3.11) New Testament Studies Volume XXXXI 1995 Cambridge University Press

Towner, P.H. "Gnosis and Realized Eschatology in Ephesus (of the Pastoral Epistles) and the Corinthian Enthusiasm." Journal for the Study of the New Testament 31 (1987): 95-124.

Towner, Philip H. "The Goal of our Instruction; The Structure of Theology and Ethics in the Pastoral Epistles". Vol 34.

Journal for the Study of the New Testament: Supplement Series, ed. David Hill. Sheffield: JSOT Press, 1989.

ABOUT THE AUTHOR

Ted Stubbersfield grew up in the small town of Gatton in Queensland, Australia in the 50's. It was a good time to be young. Life was simple, relatively safe and faith in God was taken for granted. After being thrown out of school in 1965 he started an apprenticeship as a motor mechanic, something he was ill suited to. In 1970, Ted went on an extended trip overseas and was confronted by the Christian gospel in many countries and saw for the first time that there was a God who was alive. That year he met with Jesus in a Damascus road type experience.

Ministry seemed to be the logical call on his life and he trained initially with the Church of Christ and then in the UK with the Elim Pentecostal Church but found himself most at home with a remarkable group of Grace Baptists. The Lord had mercy on His church and Ted went back to the family business, a sawmill. He kept his interest in Christian faith, living and doctrine by studying by correspondence and by writing.

Ted has a number of other publications but in a very different field, weather exposed timber structures. He is currently working as a consultant in this field.

He completed a Master of Theology in Applied Theology in 2011 through the University of Wales.